Beyond Courage

◇ *The 9 Principles of Heroism*

Chris Benguhe

A Perigee Book

P

A Perigee Book
Published by The Berkley Publishing Group
A division of Penguin Group (USA) Inc.
375 Hudson Street
New York, New York 10014

Copyright © 2003 by Chris Benguhe
Text design by Kristin del Rosario
Cover design by Ben Gibson
Cover photo copyright © Antonio Mo / Getty Images
Author photo by Scott Foust, www.scottfoust.com

First edition: June 2003

Library of Congress Cataloging-in-Publication Data

Benguhe, Chris.
Beyond courage : the 9 principles of heroism / Chris Benguhe—1st ed.
p. cm.
ISBN 0-399-52889-X
1. Heroes. I. Title.

BJ1533.H47B46 2003
179'.9—dc21   2003048085

Printed in the United States of America

10 9 8 7 6 5 4 3 2 1

Ad Majorem Dei Gloriam
And to my family, my friends and heroes everywhere.

Contents

Acknowledgments

When I glance at the cover of this book, I'm proud to see my name listed as the author. But I wish I could put the names of all those who helped me to write it smack on the cover for all to see, too.

It would take a whole other book to explain just how impossible an author's life would be without the support of family and friends. These people have been in my life for as long as I can remember, and all that I am, all that I do, and all that I aspire to do is as much because of them as it is because of any of my own efforts and ideas. My family raised me with all these principles, and they remind me of them every day of my life. My friends embody these principles in so many ways, not the least of which, keeping me well fed when times get tough. They are all my heroes, now and always. And I hope every day of my life that I am their hero, too.

Of course, this wonderful book would just be an idea in my head if it wasn't for the support and belief of my editor and publisher. Thank God for them and for all the editors and publishers in this industry who believe in books that will help us make the world a little bit lovelier.

◇ Beyond Courage

INTRODUCTION

◆ What Lies Beyond Courage?

Everyone can and should be a hero. Why? Be-cause living like a hero will yield unimaginable joy, success, and contentment for you—and for the rest of society. But at the heart of the hero mind-set is a definitive and dynamic philosophy for daily living consisting of a distinct set of principles that go well "beyond courage" and the stereotypical images of heroes we may be accustomed to seeing. This book is about how we *all* can live like heroes, and how this helps us reap the benefits of emulating those noble yet practical principles.

What you're about to read is probably a bit of a twist on what you are used to hearing about heroism in the past. The amazing stories herein exemplify the life-saving principles of everyday heroes and prove the underlying belief that our biological makeup instructs us to help each other. So only when we commit ourselves to promoting the common good through heroic living can personal triumph and fulfillment become clear and attainable. That, in turn, allows us to find the peace and strength needed to endure and overcome life's greatest challenges in the most extraordinary ways.

The heroes you'll read about here are everyday people who make miracles happen because they all believe in this distinct and dynamic philosophy of life that can be described most simply as a commitment to love. But this is not about some indefinable smultzy Hollywood version of love; rather, it is a very real and practical commitment to protect and serve humanity wherever and whenever possible. Although heroes do this for the good of others, the personal payoff is pure, unadulterated joy and contentment for themselves as well.

What Makes a Hero?

◈ *Toss out everything you've ever heard or read* about heroes now before reading this book and start fresh. Before one can understand what a hero is, it is first important to discard all the misconceptions of heroism and to understand what a hero is *not*.

For many years, most of us have listened to the modern media paint a picture of a "hero." People such as celebrities, sports icons, lottery winners, and even petty criminals were sometimes called heroes, a term based more on notoriety than merit. But these people were merely the flavor of the day, week, or month. Obviously, what these highlighted hooligans were actually being recognized for was being colorful and hugely popular. The sensational mass-market media was so obsessed with cashing in on the popular buzz, they pawned off these familiar faces as "heroic" simply because they had incredible athletic prowess, amazing fame, wealth, or some great new discovery for how to lose weight quickly and easily. They weren't and never will be heroes.

The harrowing events of September 11, 2001, changed our perception of "heroism" forever. As a slew of real heroes came on the scene, the point was driven home that these pop icons were not heroes. You'll meet several of these everyday heroes in the pages of this book.

But this brings us to yet another misconception, unfortunately once again fueled by the media, that all victims are heroes. Victims, including those unfortunate souls who perished on 9/11, can be heroes for what they did when they were alive—or even possibly for what they were doing when they died. But simply dying doesn't make them heroes. Although these individuals should be respected and revered, they are not heroes simply because of their misfortune. That doesn't make their deaths any less significant or less worthy of memorial, but trying to paint victims as heroes dilutes the meaning of the word and distorts the image of true heroes.

Neither are those who haphazardly or chaotically endanger themselves heroes—daredevils who risk life and limb for the sake of excitement, profit, or recognition. A hero is never careless with life and death because of his or her deep respect for loved ones and for the rest of the world. A hero recognizes that the world generally benefits more from his or her continued survival and success. You will never be able to truly help another human being by intentionally hurting or disrespecting yourself and your divinity.

Finally and most important, a hero is not someone who, faced with a hopeless situation, simply exercises his or her instinctual desire to survive . . . and in doing so, happens to bring about an amazing event. A man who is tied to a child and thrown into a raging river can't truly be called heroic for swimming to safety, simultaneously saving the child's life. His own simple drive to live prompted him to do so. Although his act might be courageous, the instinct for survival alone does not make him a hero. A true hero must make a moral and difficult choice to be so.

What a hero is, most simply put, is one who loves mankind and makes a moral and usually difficult decision to live a lifestyle devoted to spreading that love to the rest of society with every action and ounce of their energy. It is this philosophy of practical love and a choice to live a lifestyle of love that begets a hero. The results of that heroic life and love go well "beyond courage"—they are nothing short of miraculous for all those whose lives are touched by them.

Heroes come in all shapes and sizes, and they are found across all economic, social, religious, and cultural backgrounds. But what they all have in common is this definitive and similar

[handwritten margin note: THIS IS BEN-GUHE'S DEFINITION OF A HERO.]

4

philosophical approach to living day-to-day life. It's this loving approach that succeeds in spreading huge amounts of happiness to the world while simultaneously bringing great personal joy as well.

The Hero Lifestyle

Always remember the word lifestyle *when refer-*ring to heroes. Being a true hero is not a onetime, flash-in-the-pan event involving being in the right place at the right time and doing a good deed. Although there might be one event that brings heroes into the limelight, their heroic actions are the result of a lifetime of living, learning, and acting in accordance with that belief system that puts the value of humanity first and foremost. So often the media like to just focus on the isolated heroic events these people are involved in. But that is a great disservice to them and to the rest of us, because it deprives us from seeing the whole picture of their lives and their commitment to this philosophy of love.

More times than not, heroes have been formed by a lifelong series of difficulties or traumas that have inspired them to look at life differently, change priorities, and deepen their perspective on what the purpose of life truly is. It was only those precipitous events that demonstrated to them the power of love, whether they were on the receiving end or the giving end. Or their perspectives can be the simple result of a lifetime of prac-

[handwritten margin note: THIS IS AN IMPORTANT IDEAS: HEROES ARE NURTURED AND EMERGE OR ARISE IN A SITUATION. e.g. C.S. LEWIS ON MATH AND FORGIVENESS]

5

ticing this loving perspective on life, a perspective they learned from emulating other heroes in their life.

Now that newly formed hero is endowed with great strength, endurance, wisdom, and inspiration, which enables him to help the world around him in extraordinary ways. Heroes are hopeful and inspiring people who love the world around them in every way they can.

The fascinating by-product of this newfound devotion is that these individuals also reap the greatest and most inexplicable sense of contentment and happiness they have ever known. This contentment never deserts them, even in the toughest of circumstances. They still experience sadness, frustration, and pain, but instead of hopeless depression, they feel hopeful joy. They realize they have the ability to endure that difficulty in a heroic fashion and make something miraculous happen because of it. It is an empowering feeling.

Ultimately, what lies "beyond courage" is universal joy and peace attained through the proliferation of love. I can think of no better goal for all of us to hope for and strive toward than that. And the best part is, the hero lifestyle is one that can be cultivated. After reading the stories and thinking about the questions in this book, you, too, will be on your way to a more heroic, loving life.

CHAPTER ONE

◆ The Nine Principles of Heroism

True heroism goes beyond a single act of courage—it is a lifestyle of loving mankind every day, the effects of which ripple from each practitioner out into the world. And on occasion, that pool of goodwill produces extraordinary acts we call "heroic." The spirit of this positive lifestyle is embodied in the hero, however humble he (or his actions) might seem.

What Is Heroism?

What does heroism really mean? Doesn't every- body want to love each other? So what's so different about the way heroes look at life and love?

At its heart, the hero mind-set is a monumental shift in perspective—from a results-oriented, materialistic perspective on humanity to a humanistic, qualitative view of mankind that focuses on love itself as the desired result and goal of life. What we achieve in terms of material gains, money, and power are just tools we can use to express that love.

Since the beginning of time, mankind has had to care for each other even as pain, suffering, and hatred exists, and even as we toil to make a living by the sweat of our brow as we contend with the struggles of everyday living. Heroes understand this implicitly and accept the challenge with zeal. This separates them ideologically from others in our consumerist society, because they do not ultimately value the trivial trappings of life as much as they do the innate value of humanity.

Kant's Categorical Imperative

This desire to live a life of love is programmed inside all of us, so why don't all of us live that way all the time? There are many potential reasons why we get rewired to value material gains and success more than love, but the most prominent for us in twenty-first-century America is the Industrial Revolution.

In the early part of the twentieth century, industry taught us to replace some innate human values like love, kinship, and union with temporal values like profit, wealth, productivity, and efficiency. Assembly-line mentalities were encouraged, and people were evaluated based not on their innate human worth or how they contributed to the ultimate joy of their society or family, but instead on how well they performed on the line.

Like it or not, that mind-set has now been ingrained into

our social subconsciousness. Nowadays, many people judge their worth and base their happiness on how good they are at a simple skill or a job, how much money they make, or how perfectly they perform at one of a hundred different temporal roles. This is one of the reasons why we consistently value the rich and famous and view them as more worthy than others, because we wrongly associate quantitative success with human worth.

It's all part of the cog in the machine model of society, which says that you are only a soul-less material part of a giant machine. That means you are either a working part or a broken part, which depends not on how much you love those around you and contribute to the collective joy, but on how effectively you perform a task or fill an economic need. Consider the machinelike words we use to describe people nowadays—*dysfunctional, effective, processed*. Human beings try to behave like machines, something we were neither designed to want to do nor to do well. The result is a society in which human values become secondary at best.

But heroes buck that perspective, and see the purpose of life as serving mankind in the noblest of ways, not just for the sake of productivity. Everything they aspire to is in order to serve that purpose. And that's why they pluck at our heart strings—because they are living in the manner that we all really want to live down deep in our hearts. This doesn't mean that heroes shun or reject material items and money; rather, they see them as tools that aid or comfort them as they endeavor to love others and society. But ultimately love is the goal from which all other goals and desires in their lives are born.

Heroes act according to their human nature instead of trying to subvert that nature to the industrial mentality. People are drawn to heroes, because they are filled with the love we are all designed to want and to respond to.

Because the hero does not look at life and the lives of others as products that must be perfect, they accept flaws in themselves and others more readily. Accidents and mishaps do not inspire them to condemn others for being less than perfect. Likewise, heroes do not see life as a series of hurdles that must be "overcome" in order for happiness to be achieved; instead, they see every day as a new leg of a journey. The goal of this journey is to love others. Therefore, failure at a task or event does not make them crumble, and problems or obstacles are simply everyday occurrences that give them a chance to demonstrate their love and support of others.

The hero mentality perceives life as being about living and loving, not trying to rid one's life of what does not fit neatly and painlessly into it. But that doesn't mean heroes don't attempt to solve problems. The hero aggressively and compassionately addresses problem situations. But the goal is not to simply solve the problem like one replaces a burned-out bulb; instead, a hero seeks to confront the problem in a way that relieves the pain and suffering of those who are being affected and brings about as much common joy as possible in the process. It's living according to that age-old motto: "It's not whether you win or lose, it's how you play the game."

One of the last and most amazing aspects of heroes, one that sets them apart from many others in our society today, is that they are logically consistent in their treatment of others. The principles they exhibit toward one human being they exhibit toward all, because it is the right and naturally ordered thing to do. In other words, the hero philosophy is a complete prescription for life, not just a way to get along better with people you like in your spare time or when it's convenient for you. As you'll see in each chapter, this philosophy applies to every aspect of life—whether at home with family and friends, at the office, or even on the streets with the strangers you pass every day.

How Can I Bring Heroism into My Life?

You undoubtedly have heard and seen countless images of heroes risking death-defying odds to perform their deeds. But that's just one of the ways in which heroes give their all to live the heroic life. The stories of the everyday heroes collected in this book and the lifestyles that those heroes lead clearly delineate nine different principles to live by, namely integrity, duty, self-respect, faith, devotion, altruism, compassion, listening, and forgiveness. These powerful principles point the way for all of us to live like heroes. By emulating their lives and their devotion to these principles, we will make the world a better place. That, in a nutshell, is how and why we should all be heroes.

But if living a heroic life can be difficult, at times filled with tough choices and struggles, why should anyone really risk it? Because as heroes spread joy to others, they themselves experience the greatest joy imaginable, too. Notice I chose to use the word *joy,* not *pleasure,* because heroes might not necessarily receive self-indulgent pleasure from their heroic acts. Ultimate joy, on the other hand, may actually be found in creating happiness for others or even in events that, at face value, seem a nuisance or discomfiting to some but to the hero are joyous because of their worth to society.

The bottom line is that we all were designed to love by God. We are created to want to live a heroic life and to help others—it is what brings us joy. We are genetically predisposed to live in communities and to take care of each other. When we live according to that design, we are happier and more fulfilled. When we try to oppose that loving nature, we don't work well. We get sick, angry, hurt, and depressed. Eventually we give up, too tired to continue living against our nature, and we become isolated from society until someone else shakes us from our misdirection by loving us, thereby acting in accordance with the natural and divine design.

Heroes think people are important no matter what. And the point of life is to help those people, regardless of whether you can make that person into a productive member of society or not, whether it will garner you recognition or not, whether it will be easy or hard. That is the mark of a hero and the way to a joyful existence. That is what truly lies "beyond courage."

As you read through these chapters about these amazing but

everyday people and their incredible and valuable perspectives on life, the most important thing to remember is that these are not superheroes or figments of some Hollywood writer's mind. Nor are they saints endowed from birth with some uncommon valor or capacity to love and care for their fellow man that the rest of us don't have. These are all normal, everyday people just like you and me, who learned or were taught that to step up to the plate and love others was the smartest, most sensible, and the only reasonable and defensible way to live life. That means each one of us has the same ability to learn from these individuals a perspective on life that will allow us to live like heroes.

Sometimes it might appear as if everywhere you look nowadays you see people isolating themselves and living in cocoons of self-absorbed self-interest. Does it bother you when people walk down the street without smiling or nodding to people as they pass by? Does it disturb you when Enronlike schemers cheat and abuse their employees and stockholders? Do you wish citizens felt more responsible to each other?

The honest truth outside the world of sensational tragic headlines is that the majority of people in the world share your values and your concerns. And when people just like you stand up for those values and live accordingly, they become the heroes this book is about. We can all adopt this positive life philosophy throughout society—one hero at a time.

CHAPTER TWO

◆ The Principle of Integrity

> *"The supreme quality for leadership is unquestionably integrity. Without it, no real success is possible, no matter whether it is on a section gang, a football field, in an army, or in an office."*
>
> —Dwight David Eisenhower,
> thirty-fourth United States president

Think back to the Clinton-Lewinsky scandal of the late 1990s, when all the country was abuzz trying to decide whether or not the president actually had an affair with Monica Lewinsky. Then he came out very publicly to quiet the scandal by telling us he didn't. When it came to light that Clinton had lied, or at least grossly affected the truth, the entire country tried to decide whether or not he should resign or, worse still, be impeached.

Now, remember another U.S. presidential administration, when President George Bush went on TV and vowed, "No new taxes." When he went back on his word and raised taxes, some say this flip-flop cost him re-election.

Regardless of your particular politics, the fact that his acts of dishonesty could have ended Clinton's presidency (and that

Bush was not re-elected) is telling. It was the voters' way of saying to these politicians, "We want you to be a man of your word. We value integrity, and you should, too!"

Our society still values honesty and integrity, almost above all else. Even in this skeptical day and age, when journalists and comedians make a living betting on the deceit of politicians, we, the people, still hold up honesty and integrity as a goal we want our leaders to strive for.

Do you mean what you say? Are you honest? Do you keep promises? Do you follow through on commitments? Do you think it's important to be a man or woman of your word?

Oaths; promises; commitments to friends, colleagues, customers, or clients; marriage vows; and just plain everyday honesty are some of the ways we in the modern world show our integrity and give our word or commitment to another human being. But how important is it for us to stay true to this principle nowadays?

The concept of integrity is at the core of the concept of heroism. In fact, it is the very most basic and primary principle from which all the other elements of heroism and living a heroic life must grow out of, because if you aren't able to commit your word, you aren't capable of committing your life and actions to any principles of behavior, either. A lifetime commitment to earnestness is first and foremost necessary. But integrity can be a tough principle to live sometimes. What price would *you* be willing to pay for your integrity?

What Is Integrity?

Today, many once-valued commitments strike us as outdated or trivial. We seem to find it almost impossible to believe that anyone could make a lifelong commitment to anything or anyone. The concept of an "oath" doesn't get much attention nowadays, but it was once an integral part of life. Oaths of office now seem more like quaint traditions than a real and binding promise. And a doctor's Hippocratic oath to comfort and heal his patients tends to take a backseat in importance to the legal liabilities of malpractice.

In our own daily lives, how trite has the phrase "I promise" become? We say it every day, perhaps dozens of times. "I promise I'll call you." "I promise that's true." "I promise the check is in the mail." "I promise the delivery will be there tomorrow." "I promise I'll be there." But few of us lose much sleep when we break that cavalier commitment. Even marriage vows are frequently taken for granted—"To love, honor, and obey" can turn into "I'll think about you when I can find the time."

Integrity means making a promise and sticking to it. In a world more and more accustomed to comfort and leisure, the concept of holding fast to a principle, regardless of the difficulty or discomfort, proves less popular. Heroes know better than anyone that their commitment to honesty and to keeping their word might sometimes put them at odds with the concerns and temptations of the everyday world. They might have to choose

Psalm 15:4

17

between comfort and conscience when times get tough, submitting themselves to conflict and humiliation in order to keep their integrity intact. But in the end, a heroic commitment to your word delivers a fuller and more rewarding life.

Yet even more important than the personal rewards of integrity are the benefits for society. The very fabric of civilization depends on integrity. Think about it for a second. Just about every important institution, service, and foundation in our society would cease to function correctly if it weren't for the element of integrity in individuals. Consider a hospital where the doctors no longer adhered to their Hippocratic oath to heal, but instead only thought about bringing in greater fees for themselves or the hospital by lying and performing unnecessary procedures or surgeries. Think of a police force that no longer thought it was important to fulfill their obligation to protect and serve the citizens, instead opting to use their position in society to serve selfish desires for power and control. What if politicians and judges no longer felt it necessary to respect their promise to uphold the Constitution of the Unites States, because they just didn't feel like it? What about something as simple as families—imagine a marriage in which spouses aren't honest with each other and where infidelity is the norm, or where children see no reason to be truthful to their parents.

Integrity is one of the basic building blocks of civilization and humanity. It's the method by which we all fulfill our social contract with each other—to live in a society instead of just living according to our base, animal instincts. As members of modern society, we agree to abide by those values. If it wasn't for integrity, we could break our word to obey any laws in the U.S. Constitution. If all that was stopping us was the fear of punishment, there wouldn't be enough police officers and judges to process the criminals! The truth is that most of us behave because we believe it is right to be honest, and we keep our unspoken word to each other to live lawfully.

And on a personal level, integrity is the building block of our own personal triumph. Just as Eisenhower said, one needs to be a person of integrity to be good at anything else. Integrity leads to greater happiness and success at work, as colleagues respect you more and look to you for leadership and guidance. Integrity leads to deeper, more meaningful, and more dependable friendships and relationships, as friends and family members trust you more. You garner greater respect and support in your community for being a person of integrity, valor, and honesty. And integrity leads to greater physical health and peace of mind, because you are not saddled with the guilt and worries of keeping track of lies and deceptions.

On the other hand, a lack of integrity isolates you and distances you from the rest of society. Nobody likes to hang out with someone who they can't trust. Nobody wants to work with somebody who they can't depend on.

How Can I Bring a Sense of Integrity into My Life?

The way to being an honest person of integrity isn't hard to understand. In fact, it really requires no explanation at all. It is the simple act of responding to conscience. Most of us know the difference between the truth and a lie, and most of us know that when we make a promise, we should keep it. Any further explanation of those simple concepts would just muddy the water. These codicils make it that much easier to rationalize lying and dishonor by adding all kinds of stipulations as to when and where and why you didn't have to stick to what you said. I'll leave those rationalizations up to you.

Now, nobody can be perfect all the time, and leading a heroic life is not about being perfect. It's easy to find ourselves slipping down the path of deceit and dishonor occasionally. It's not hard to make a mistake. But in the end, it comes down to standing up and telling the truth, keeping your word when others are depending on you to do so, even though it might cost you. Remembering that part about "when others are depending on you" is the key to finding the extra strength you need to have that integrity. If we constantly remind ourselves that integrity is not so much about "keeping a promise," but instead about our responsibility to love others by respecting their right to our honesty, it becomes a little easier to do the right thing. Simply put, lying or not keeping our word breaks the bond we have formed with others and with society. It tells others that we do not believe they are worthy of our respect, and eventually it inspires others to lie or break their words to us. Reminding ourselves of that should go a long way to help us have integrity.

Although many industries and sectors of society today seem to be devaluing integrity, it is now and always will be alive and well in the human soul because it is so basic to our happiness. And acts of integrity continually surprise and inspire us with their ability to change the world—even in the most unlikely places.

- Key members of the Nixon White House risked everything to honestly answer questions to a couple nosy reporters named Woodward and Bernstein . . . and eventually, many told the truth to Congress, exposing the corruption of the presidency of Richard Nixon.

- Structural engineer William LeMessurier admitted that his firm might have mistakenly made a potentially catastrophic design flaw when building the famous fifty-nine-story Citicorp Tower in New York City in 1977 . . . even though nobody would have been the wiser had he said nothing. When an architecture student brought the flaw to his attention, LeMessurier immediately fixed the problem at great costs to his firm, potentially saving many lives in the process. Amazingly, even though the mistake cost his liability insurance company millions, they rewarded him by lowering his insurance premiums. They were so impressed with his integrity that they saw him as less of a risk in the future.

Finally, here is the incredibly inspiring story of Brett Roby, a quality engineer who risked it all to save the lives of young men and women he never knew and would never meet. It's the story that proves that somewhere and somehow, people's lives depend on our integrity.

MISSION ACCOMPLISHED

[handwritten: re: the Helicopter problem // Ford Pinto problem]

Thirty-seven-year-old Brett Roby was a quality engineer for the firm of Speco Corporation in Springfield, Ohio, in 1993. He had plenty of problems and hardships on his plate. Following his divorce, he was adjusting as well as could be expected. And his affliction with Ryder's Syndrome, an incurable and life-threatening form of arthritis caused by inflammation of the connective tissue, was progressing rapidly, making it tougher and tougher to get through the day.

But he had worked himself up to a level of respect in the company, and he was excited about the future. There was a bright spot, too—his assignment of testing parts for the Army's Chinook helicopter. It was a job he loved.

"I might not have been the best quality engineer in the world," Brett said with characteristic humbleness. "There were those who were better or smarter than me, but I always did the best I could and I believed in what I was doing. When you hire somebody, you hire him for his conscience as well as his mind—especially when you are working in a job that deals with people's lives."

Growing up in a family of seven in Arkansas with a salesman dad and a stay-at-home mom, Brett was always instructed by his parents to work hard and follow his heart. "If you believe you're right, then you have to go with it," his dad always used to tell him. But he never thought adhering to that advice would one day cost him his job and leave him broke. He also didn't realize it could one day save so many lives.

Speco Corporation made transmission gears for the Army's Boeing CH-47D Chinook transport helicopters, a workhorse of a chopper capable of carrying thirty-three personnel. Brett's job was to make sure the gears, which were designed by Boeing, worked the way they were supposed to. But something wasn't quite right—the helicopters were failing. A couple crashes in the early 1990s luckily did not result in any fatalities, but another Chinook with similarly designed gears made by another company went down in Honduras in 1988, killing all five crew members.

Brett didn't know if all the crashes were related to the gears, but he was determined to find out what was wrong. It would be a disaster if one helicopter went down filled with personnel during an important mission. "We started to do metal tests on the gears, and what we found wasn't good," reveals Brett. "There were terrible problems with the metal of the gears overheating under stress. These gears were critical to the flight of the aircraft. This needed to be addressed immediately because lives were at stake, and just about all the testing personnel I gave this to agreed."

But the moment he started to suggest that there might be a problem, Brett began getting the brush-off. At first he assumed it might just be the normal reaction to a quality inspector's objections. Brett knew being a quality assurance engineer was never the most popular job in any company. Hard-working and well-intentioned designers, craftsmen, and laborers worked hard to make a product, and the last thing they wanted to hear was that it wasn't working.

"To a lot of people, the quality people are like the enemy," says Brett. "They are working with you, but they don't necessarily feel like you're part of the same team. I didn't have anything against any of those hard-working people, but I had a job to do, and that was to assure the safety of that product."

So Brett did his job, and when people at his own level didn't seem interested in fixing the problem, he reported it to his superiors. He realized his findings would not be music to anyone's ears, but at least he figured the problems would be fixed. But to Brett's shock and surprise, he was told not to worry about it and simply to declare the gears safe and sound. "Nobody wanted to talk about this at all," says Brett. "So I just kept going up the ladder. I figured eventually somebody in this company must want to know about this."

But the higher he went and the more noise he made, the

more resistance he met. Soon Brett started to feel like this was not just mere indifference. He heard rumblings about his job being on the line if he didn't stop making waves. But Brett continued with his tests of the gears, and every test confirmed his worst fears—that the metal the gears were made of, a proprietary metal Boeing insisted be used, just wasn't holding up. Brett knew that if he didn't get somewhere with this people were going to die soon.

Getting nowhere in his company, Brett contacted people at Boeing to alert them to the problem, hoping someone there would do something about it. But again to his surprise, he was informed that they felt there was no problem with the gears, and that he should forget this whole issue. "People kept telling me to stop looking into this," reveals Brett. "They ordered me to discontinue the tests, but I wasn't going to just lie down on this, because I knew it was important. But when I tried to work on it, I found out my requests for testing weren't honored."

Eventually, everyone at Brett's company and at Boeing was ordered to stop testing on the gears. It was pretty clear to the well-intentioned engineer at that point that this was a money issue. "It was going to mean real dollars to fix this," says Brett, "and they didn't want to hear about that."

Brett didn't know what to do, and the stress of it all wasn't helping his condition. As the pressure mounted, he got sicker and sicker. But he wouldn't give up, even as the rumors of him getting fired grew louder and louder. Brett had a job to do, and he was going to do it. There were lives depending on it, and it was eating him up inside. "You can pack a lot of people on those 'copters," says Brett. "I was really bugged that the bottom line seemed to be more important to the company than the safety of those people. We all make mistakes, but how many of us get the chance to fix those mistakes in time to save lives?" Brett knew that sticking to his guns was a matter of life and death.

Brett didn't know what to do or where to turn. With everyone telling him to look the other way, his job on the line, and his health faltering, he started to doubt himself and his stubborn insistence. He wondered whether he should just "go with the flow" and give up the fight. Every day Brett questioned himself and his motives.

But every time he turned on the TV and saw a news report on the military, he thought about those young men and women who would be risking life and limb on those helicopters. He saw those fresh young faces with their whole lives ahead of them. Their lives were hanging in the balance, and now Brett's integrity was the only thing that could save them. "These transport helicopters were being loaded up with human beings," says Brett. "These military men and women who were really just kids were risking their lives to protect us, and it was our job to assure their safety and the safety of the pilots onboard that vehicle. I couldn't pretend these gears were safe when I knew in my heart they weren't. How could I let men and women get into a vehicle with an inherently flawed component? I wouldn't do it."

Brett loved his job, he needed the salary, plus he liked the people he worked with. But he knew his first and foremost responsibility was the safety of those soldiers. Once Brett decided he was going all the way with his fight, he realized it would take drastic measures to get anything done. While continuing to try and make in roads within the company, he decided he needed help—big help.

He took his test results—and his fight—to the federal government. The day he made that decision was one of the hardest days of his life. He knew that now there was no tuning back, no matter how long the struggle or how hard the fight. "I knew it was probably career suicide," says Brett. "I was betting it all." And sure enough, when word got out that he went to the feds, his life changed forever.

Brett's first stop on his long road was to the Defense Criminal Investigations Services of the federal government. Considering the gravity of the complaint, they immediately began researching his claim. But until they could make a case and make something happen, it was business as usual for Boeing and Speco, and it was back to work for Brett.

It wasn't an easy task. Everywhere he went in the company he would hear the whispers and rumors behind his back. He thought it was just a matter of time before he got the ax. But in the meantime, the government wanted him to gather as much information as he could that would help make the case, a task that didn't come naturally to the mild-mannered engineer. "Right after I went to the government I heard that the company was trying to figure out a way to get rid of me if I didn't stop making trouble," remembers Brett, "but the government told me to keep them informed. So on one hand I was trying hard to keep my job because I couldn't afford to get fired, but on the other I was trying to find out information. It was the most stressful situation I'd ever experienced in my entire life and certainly something I was never prepared for."

As the government's investigation progressed, Brett did his part keeping them abreast of information on the gears while still trying to convince people in his company and Boeing to reconsider retesting the gears. In a last-ditch effort to convince them, he attended a meeting between Speco and Boing bigwigs. The government asked Brett to attend the meeting, go undercover, and wear a wire to tape the conversation.

"It was terrifying," says Brett. "In all my life I never thought this was something I was going to be doing." It was something straight out of a TV cop show, except this was for real. Brett wasn't ready for it. "I worked hard to make a career for myself and to do a good job," says Brett, "but because I cared about my job, I was going to lose it, and now I was wearing a wire to catch my colleagues. The whole situation was horrible, but there was no other way. I couldn't back out now."

Brett had one last hope that maybe the meeting was a chance to get everything out on the table. He might finally be able to convince the Boeing people that these gears needed to be redesigned. Maybe there was still a chance that he could convince them to do the right thing. But just in case he couldn't, he wore the wire like the government asked. It was the last thing he wanted to think was necessary. But now it was up to them.

That day, as Brett made the long walk toward the boardroom to discuss the problem with representatives from both Speco and Boeing, he was a nervous wreck. The stress of the last few weeks was inflaming his medical condition and fatigue. He could feel the pain shooting through every joint in his body as he thought of what he was about to do. A million reasons why he should back out rushed through his head, but the image of those young military faces outweighed them all.

Still, he hoped that maybe once and for all when he told the higher-ups at Boeing what was happening, they wouldn't stand for it. Maybe the government investigation wouldn't be necessary. But Brett's hopes were dashed the moment he walked into the meeting. "It was absolutely not to be discussed ever again," reveals Brett. "It was made very clear to me right then and there that this was no longer an issue, and I was to stop pursuing this or I would certainly lose my job."

Shortly after that meeting, Brett found himself out of work. With no job, no income, and nowhere else to turn, he went back home to live with his mom in Arkansas, hoping to get his head straight and figure out what to do next. Being back home reminded him of all the reasons why he did what he did. Although he was nervous about the future, he felt good about the past. "I knew I did what was right," says Brett. "It's the way I was taught as a child to live. My mother reminded me of that when I asked her what she thought about the whole thing. There are more important things than money. There is the value of human lives, and those are worth more than any price you can pay." And

29

finally for Brett, there was a value on integrity, which super-seded economic issues. "There is so much more to life than the bottom line," says Brett.

Broke, sick, and fired, there wasn't much more Brett could do now to try to remedy the situation and save those lives . . . or was there? When he heard about a law firm that specialized in situations like his, Brett gave them a call to see if there was any-thing more he could do on his own. "I must admit that I wasn't very hopeful at the time," says Brett. But what the lawyers told him was earth-shattering. Brett could sue Speco for wrongful termination to try to help out with his medical bills, but more important, he could sue Boeing under an old law called the False Claims Act of 1863. The law allows private citizens to file suit against someone on behalf of the federal government if they believe the government is being defrauded. It could make Boe-ing fix the flawed gear design he felt was endangering people.

"Here was a way to get those choppers to stop flying until they were safe," says Brett. "And that's all I really wanted." For the first time, his lawyers gave him hope. "You don't usually hear too much praise of lawyers nowadays," says Brett, "but when they said they were ready to fight for this, they gave me the strength I needed to keep going."

Brett and his new legal team immediately filed the suit, which they invited the federal government to join. But this was no fast fix. For the next two years, the government did their homework, conducting hundreds of tests, studies, and interviews before finally deciding to get onboard. In the meantime, Brett's health was quickly deteriorating. With no money for his rising medical bills and little more than low-wage jobs available to the now-famous whistleblower, he was beginning to wonder if he would eventually come to regret his costly integrity. "It was really starting to look bleak," reveals Brett. "The case kept dragging on, and I didn't know if I was ever going to be able to make anything happen. But my lawyers never let me lose hope."

The hard-nosed government attorneys together with Brett's personal lawyers fought tooth and nail. In the midst of it all, Speco went out of business, leaving Boeing as the sole defender. Again and again, Boeing claimed they had done nothing wrong, that the gears were fine, and that the crashes weren't related. Brett watched them do all they could to discredit his findings and his competency. But 300 depositions and millions of pages of documentation turned up more and more damning evidence.

According to the government, documents showed Boeing knew about the flawed design in 1985, when it installed the disputably designed part onto the Chinook helicopter. This helicopter crashed three years later on a hillside near La Cieba, Honduras, killing five soldiers. Brett later discovered that many other employees also knew about the flawed parts and wanted to come forward, too, but they were afraid they would lose their jobs. In fact, Speco's president himself even said in a deposition that he believed Boeing's design was flawed, but was pressured by Boeing to keep quiet or else lose the contract. He testified that their callousness caused his company to go out of business.

The case was now in the hands of attorneys, and Brett tried to hang on to his health while they fought the good fight. He prepared himself for the long court case that was to come and wished there was some way he could get those helicopters out of the sky in the meantime. Then his wish came true.

Faced with mountains of evidence, Boeing finally decided to settle the case in August 2000. As part of the settlement, the military grounded 388 of the helicopters and ordered them refitted with redesigned gears to ensure their safety. The federal government was awarded $61 million in damages, and Brett received $10 million of that for his part in bringing the case forward. It was an unexpected and remarkable reward for telling the truth when all the cards were stacked against him.

"I knew in my heart what was going on was wrong," says Brett, "and I couldn't just cover it up. All I wanted to see was the helicopters get fixed so I could ensure the safety of those men and women. I've done that. Maybe I saved some lives."

A few months later, Brett got a phone call from a new friend who called to tell him how much she appreciated him risking his job to tell the truth. It was Patricia Kropp, the mother of one of the five soldiers killed in the helicopter crash in Honduras twelve years before. "That really was indescribable for me, because it put a name, a face, and even a voice on the whole thing," says Brett. Patricia had called Brett to thank him on behalf of all the moms who, because of him, now would never have to go through what she did. "There were lots of mothers out there of those kids who were risking their lives for their country," says Brett, "and they had a right to expect me to do my job honestly. They deserved my integrity."

After paying all his bills and legal expenses, Brett wound up with $3.5 million. He gave half a million to a very special private school in Florida that teaches the values of integrity and helping your fellow man as an important part of the curriculum. "I still believe people inherently want to do the right thing," says Brett, "but maybe if we teach all our children to live their lives honestly, people won't ever have to go through what I had to do in order to do the right thing. Wouldn't that be a nice dream to see happen?"

CHAPTER THREE

◆ The Principle of Duty

excellent
re: duty

> *"O, good old man, how well in thee appears*
> *The constant service of the antique world,*
> *When service sweat for duty, not for mead!*
> *Thou art not for the fashion of these times,*
> *Where none will sweat but for promotion."*
>
> —William Shakespeare, *As You Like It*

Have you counted the number of casinos in this country lately? Or tallied up how many lottery drawings are held each week from coast to coast? And then there are those get-rich-quick schemers on late-night TV who don't just promise you prosperity—they want to make you *so* rich that you'll never have to do anything ever again but sit on your duff. Never before in this country have there been so many ways to make money so quickly and so many people willing to do just about anything to hit it big and never work again.

Once, the so-called American Dream was getting a great job that would allow you to earn the money to buy a nice house and a comfortable, happy life for your family. But the new American Dream seems to be based more on wealth than happiness. This preoccupation with wealth, no matter how it is attained, undermines one of the most important and basic reasons for work—to do our duties by serving the needs of our communities.

There is nothing inherently wrong with money when it is a representation of the worth of a service or product to society. When you serve society in some valuable way, society traditionally reimburses you for that contribution with money. The desire to make more money for your hard work is a good one. It probably means that you value what you do, which means you will work hard at it, and you believe that others should value your effort enough to pay you fairly for it. And there's certainly nothing wrong with the average retired couple heading out to the casino with a few spare bucks for the thrill of hearing those little buzzers go off when they hit the big jackpot.

But for many in this country, the need for more and more money (and the complete disregard for how we obtain it) is completely separated from our desire to serve society. Once we stop seeing money as our reward for contributing to society but instead simply as something we need to survive—regardless of how we obtain it—we become scavengers. At that point, we are little more than animals foraging in the jungles of modern-day cities, ready to do anything for our food. If we approve of this kind of socially irresponsible perspective on earning a living, how do we explain to young people the importance of hard honest work or why it's wrong to steal or commit crimes for quick cash? We can't.

What Is Duty?

Every time you turn on one of those great old war movies, at one point or another the hero talks about his or her duty. It's usually some suicide mission or gravely difficult task they must perform to save the world. But outside Hollywood histrionics, what does the concept of duty mean? And more important, what does it mean to us in our day-to-day lives?

Once while speaking to a group of high-school students I asked the question, "What is duty?" The myriad misguided answers I received was startling. Many suggested it meant something that you must do, some disdainful task that you didn't want to perform. This was hardly the noble definition of duty I was looking for.

Spurred on by this, I put the question to a wide range of adults. Very few offered suggestions. Maybe that's because outside military applications, the word has all but lost its use in modern society. Those who made an effort defined duty as responsibility. But there is a great and important divide between the two words and what they mean in everyday life. Responsibility implies taking care of one's own needs. But duty is a far nobler and inclusive term, one which implies morally conscious service to *others*.

Duty, or an obligation to serve, is an approach to living. It is a humanistic belief that life is not just about taking care of one's

Here duty is defined.

needs such as food and shelter, but also about fulfilling a grander purpose with everything one does. That purpose is to love and help others. The special individuals who demonstrate this philosophy in their remarkable day-to-day lives are heroes because they feel a sense of mission or a moral obligation to the rest of society.

This passionate perspective on life translates into every aspect of their daily life. When they call someone a friend, it is a commitment to help and foster that person. They are dedicated to their families through thick and thin, whether it is convenient for them to do so or not. And their commitment to doing their jobs is not just about making a living but about doing their duty and making a meaningful difference in the world.

We must all face the challenge of menial tasks, obstacles, and the responsibilities of making money every day. But heroes also see the duty of their work as an opportunity to serve, regardless of their job. Whether a shoe salesman or a surgeon, a forest ranger or a fireman, heroes find a purpose beyond money that motivates them, that inspires them to surpass the requirements of the job. The most significant result of this attitude is that quite often they change and even save lives in the process, and humanity is served in the greatest of ways.

But the secondary result of their actions and their attitudes is that they experience extremely high job satisfaction and they are able to incorporate their occupations into the grand scheme of their life, which helps them avoid becoming heartless zombies. They don't suffer the need to hate their jobs eight hours a day, then come home and try to "chill" in front of the TV for several hours before they can be pleasant for their friends and families. The result is a happier and healthier self, never wearying from the rigors of everyday life but instead inspired by life's challenges.

How Can I Bring a Sense of Duty into My Life?

Although doing your duty isn't always easy, it's not hard to figure out how to do it. Breaking the mold of mindless and meaningless individualism and egocentric existence can best be accomplished by reminding yourself that life is about making a difference, not just a living. You can make a difference working in almost any occupation, provided it's not one that pits you against humanity, in which case maybe it's time to look elsewhere for employment. Adopting a perspective that somewhere, somehow, somebody's life might depend on you doing your duty will add an entire new dimension to your job and your life.

Those who choose to live as heroes become instilled with almost superhuman strength to face everyday challenges because of this different perspective. Because they are not only focused on their own success but instead on serving the common good, personal obstacles and challenges are not taken as signs of failure. The very act of trying to help others makes them a success.

[handwritten: This is Jacob Marley's admonition to Ebenezer Scrooge.]

39

It's all about the process of contributing and trying to help. And if you are accomplishing that, then you are a success. Then you are doing your duty and you have the right to be proud of it.

That was the case with two very special men who lived their entire lives serving their family, friends, and the rest of society with everything they did, and especially through their occupations. They so perfectly embodied the principle of duty every day of their lives by inspiring and helping others in many ways . . . and they eventually saved many lives because of it. Both of these men lost their lives on September 11, 2001, but their stories and their legacies stand as a memorial, reminding us all to do our duty, whatever it is, as if somewhere, somehow, somebody's life might depend on it.

JUST DOING THEIR JOBS

On September 11, 2001, two hardworking family men woke up just like millions of other New Yorkers did that day. They showered, dressed, ate their morning breakfast, kissed their spouses good-bye, and headed off for work. These two men never met, although they worked only a few miles apart every day and within a few hours they would be fighting the same fight to save the lives of thousands of people trapped inside the doomed towering infernos once known as the World Trade Center.

Retired Army Colonel Cyril Richard Rescorla and FDNY Lieutenant Timothy Stackpole came from completely different worlds. Rick was an expatriated British soldier who lived hard and traveled the world establishing a storied past for himself. He joined America's fight in the blood-and-guts battles of Vietnam, where he distinguished himself as a no-nonsense leader who dove full-steam ahead into deadly confrontations when he had to in order to save others. After Vietnam, Rick moved to the United States, became a citizen, and led a kinder and gentler life as a college professor, then a security expert and a family man.

Tim, on the other hand, was a good Irish Brooklyn boy who grew up, went to church, got married, and worked as a New York firefighter, all within about a square mile or two of the block he was born.

Yet as different as these two heroes' backgrounds were, their goals and motives were strikingly similar and led them to the same place on that fateful day. Both did their duty every day of their lives as if the world was depending on them. Both men were just everyday people, not celebrities in the least, but they lived with extraordinary valor. They both talked about their jobs not as if it was some burdensome task to perform for a paycheck, but as if those jobs were opportunities to help others in amazing ways. And neither Rick nor Tim was supposed to be at work on September 11, but both men often took on extra shifts to help others, and they did so that day, with no way of knowing what was about to transpire.

Rick Rescorla always wanted to be a hero. It's the way he always thought people were supposed to want to live. He read literary tales of heroes like those in Kipling's *The Man Who Would Be*

King, and he researched heroes like World War II soldier Audie Murphy for a screenplay he wrote about the famous Medal of Honor winner. Rescorla himself was an instrumental part of the incredible heroic events chronicled in the book *We Were Soldiers,* about the miraculous survival of the U.S. 7th Cavalry facing insurmountable odds in a key battle during the Vietnam War. The book was subsequently made into the 2002 movie starring Mel Gibson.

From the time Rick was young he wanted to help—he wanted to go where the action was, and he wanted to contribute in whatever way he could. Born in the rough working-class seaport town of Hayle, England, Rick never knew his father, but he had all the love he needed from his mom and grandparents. He was a natural born leader who took control on the rugby field, and his peers respected him for his courage and street smarts. Rick was the kind of man who knew what to do and felt it was his responsibility to help others see it, too.

Ready to make a difference, the rugged teenager signed up with the British Paratroopers when he was only sixteen years old, and later joined Her Majesty's Colonial Force in Rhodesia. Then he returned home to England, where he worked for England's famed Scotland Yard. When Rick was twenty-four years old, America was just getting involved in Vietnam, so although still a British citizen, he joined the U. S. Army to do what he believed was right—help fight communism in Southeast Asia with the American forces. His command experience proved invaluable, and he was made a second lieutenant after basic training and given his own platoon in Bravo Company of the 2nd Battalion of the 7th Cavalry.

As the movie *We Were Soldiers* dramatically depicts, American soldiers were surrounded by enemy troops at a landing zone they called X-Ray in November 1965. There, in the thick overgrowth of the Ia Drang Valley, American commander Lieutenant Colonel Hal Moore lost more than 100 men during the first day of fighting. He was greatly outnumbered by the enemy, almost ten to one. Rick's unit was ordered in to help defend the perimeter against thousands of enemy troops. He quickly went to work thinking of how to keep his men alive against the onslaught that was bound to come. He instructed his men to dig foxholes while he sneaked across enemy lines to see what the enemy could see, returning with vital strategic information that would make the difference between survival and annihilation. That night, Rick and his men hung on and endured wave after wave of attacks while Rick sang songs to his troops to keep them from falling apart.

The next day his company was evacuated, and they thought the worst was over. But when the rest of the battalion was ambushed, Rick and his unit were sent back in to the hell they had just escaped to rescue them. Although once again severely outnumbered, Rick and his company came to the rescue. Airdropped into the middle of a combat zone, Rick himself leapt from a crashing chopper under fire to assure wearied soldiers that together they would prevail. He took every death of every man under his command that day seriously, holding their hands when possible while they took their last breaths. All told, more than 300 American soldiers and 3,000 Vietnamese fighters died during that first major battle of the Vietnam conflict. The fighting was so fierce and the result so ghastly, that the place was renamed for posterity The Valley of Death.

Rick Rescorla left Vietnam with a Silver Star, a Purple Heart, Bronze stars for Valor and Meritorious Service, and a battered French army bugle that the North Vietnamese had wrested from the French and he had recaptured as a symbol of victory for the United States.

Through all that time and through all his bravery, courage, and heroism, Rick didn't think he was doing anything too special. He just believed he was doing his duty—his mission was to help and save others while compromising the enemy. And he wasn't even particularly proud of his military exploits themselves, telling friends years later that when the top brass lost sight of the goal of defeating communism, he lost sight of the reason for that war. What he was proud of, though, was his never-ending commitment to doing his duty and saving the lives of his men.

After leaving Vietnam, Rick became an American citizen and finished his Army stint in 1968 in Fort Benning, Georgia. Then he attended the University of Oklahoma, where he studied creative writing and earned his bachelor's and master's degrees in literature. He went onto law school—not necessarily what one might expect from a military warrior! But once again, Rick's intentions were not to be a general, but to be a hero who did his duty. And now he was looking for his next mission in the civilian world.

Rick decided to use his law degree to teach criminal justice, and he was always as much of an inspiration to his students as he was to his men on the battlefield. His deep, powerful, and assuring voice inspired listening and learning as much as it inspired leadership in battle. He married in 1972 and had two children, and he enjoyed the fruits of family life. Teaching was rewarding for Rick, and he did his job with all the honor and dedication that he always did his duty. But the ivory tower of college academia made him feel as if he was doing a great deal of talking but not much doing. He found his next mission a few years later as a security expert for a series of banks and brokerage houses before landing with Dean Witter around 1985. His mission was to safeguard their home offices in the World Trade Center.

Once again, Rick's job was more than just a paycheck. It was his chance to help others with every fiber of his being. His superiors and his colleagues were constantly surprised by how much he cared about his job. He worked diligently to make the building, especially the twenty-two floors his company occupied, as safe as he could. He worked long hours into the night, studying the design of the building and how to make it invulnerable to any kind of attack or incursion. He drew up countless evacuation plans to make sure that in the event a catastrophe did happen, everyone could get out in time to prevent any deaths.

Long into the night Rick could be seen walking the halls, checking all the nooks and crannies in the building for any detail he might have missed, any possible breach of security or weak spot. He even brought in one of his old Army buddies who was an expert on antiterrorism to advise him on how he thought the building might be vulnerable so the company could prepare better. Years before the 1993 bombing of the World Trade Center, Rick warned that the basement was the building's soft spot and that the greatest threat to the building at that time was an underground truck bomb. Sadly, his prediction came true when terrorists drove a truck filled with explosives into the garage and detonated it. After it happened, there was Rick, jumping on top of a desk with a bullhorn to get the panicky crowd's attention so he could get people out of the building quickly and safely. As always, seeing his job as a matter of duty, Rick refused to leave until the entire tower was empty.

Things didn't work out with his first wife, but they remained good friends. She still impresses all those who ask with extraordinary but true tales of her ex-husband's compassion and concern for others, like the way he used to always chip in to help neighbors with their chores even after a long day, or the way he might take a sleeping bag to a homeless man or buy someone a meal. At work he was the backbone of morale, giving co-workers a reason to believe they were safe in the towering skyscraper when many feared to return to work after the 1993 bombing.

Rick met his second wife in 1998, and they embarked on a whirlwind romance that changed her life. "He was an amazing man who lived to help others," says Susan Rescorla. "You could especially hear it in his voice. It was so strong and in command, but not because he was trying to boss you around. It was because he wanted to show you where to go. He made you feel safe."

Rick continued to make the people at Morgan Stanley Dean Witter feel safe. He perfected evacuation plans and insisted on holding fire drills every few months—even when top brass said it wasn't needed and even when employees moaned over the rote and repetitive exercises. He insisted on being prepared. Always trying to stay one step ahead of catastrophes for the sake of those he was there to protect, once again Rick studied the building and its weaknesses. He warned that the next attack would come from the skies in the form of a rogue cargo plane filled with explosives or chemical or biological weapons, and that its impact could bring down one or both of the towers.

If that had been the end of Rick Rescorla's life, still what a remarkable life it would have been, filled with all the attributes of heroism, a life lived for duty. But there was still one final, important chapter to be written in Rick's saga of selflessness. It was the ultimate fitting conclusion to a life lived for others. He still had to make the people he worked for feel safe one more time.

On September 11, 2001, Rick Rescorla dressed for work in his dark blue suit, singing a happy tune and entertaining his wife with impressions of one of his favorite actors, Anthony Hopkins. He wasn't even supposed to be going into the office that day—he was getting ready to go abroad to attend his daughter's wedding—but when a colleague needed time off for personal reasons, he agreed to fill in. He grabbed his wife around the waist and spun her around for a little dance, then he gave her a big kiss good-bye and told her he loved her. Susan kissed him back, telling him that she didn't need any movie star because she had him.

He was in his office on the forty-fourth floor of the South Tower by 8 A.M. Just like every morning, the office was abuzz with people he needed to see and things that needed to be done yesterday, but like always, Rick took a moment to call his wife on the phone to tell her he loved her. About forty-five minutes later, the first plane crashed into the North Tower.

As people across the nation, the city, and in the towers themselves scrambled frantically to figure out what was happening, Port Authority Police said that everything was under control and instructed people in the South Tower to stay put until further notice. But Rick knew it was up to him to save the lives of the people in his company. He had prepared for this, and he was ready to do what he was there and paid to do—to keep those people safe.

He immediately ordered the evacuation of all floors under his control, floors forty-four through seventy-four. That meant clearing 2,700 employees out of the building while abruptly telling Port Authority Police that their assessment of the safety of the situation was dead wrong. He warned them that they should get the rest of the building out before the whole thing came down. After all, Rick practically predicted this entire scenario so far, and he had no reason to doubt that the rest of his prediction would play out. He was sure the buildings would collapse. He didn't have much time to do his duty.

While his employees funneled out of the building in an orderly fashion, just as he had trained them to do so many times before, Rick sang Cornish inspirational songs to comfort them just as he did in Vietnam. No longer the young and physically agile warrior he once was, the heavyset sixty-one-year-old man still pushed himself to the limit as he ran back and forth from floor to floor making sure each and every one was out. Unlike most of the rest the building, almost all of Morgan Stanley's employees were already out of the South Tower when the second plane hit at a little after 9 A.M.

As the shattered tower went black, the thousands of employees below the seventy-first floor (where the plane hit) scurried to get out. People above that floor frantically leapt for their lives from windows to avoid burning to death. But most of Morgan Stanley's people were watching the horror from outside the buildings—all except for Rick and the few security people who stood by his side.

Rick stayed, heading upward toward the flames when all were coming down to make sure everyone was gone. Floor by floor he checked offices, helped stragglers, and motivated people who he wasn't even paid to protect. In the midst of all the mayhem, he made a call to his wife. "If something happens to me, I want you to know you made my life," were his final words to her.

In all, only six Morgan Stanley employees died that day—

including Rick Rescorla—and it was all because of one man who chose to see his job as a mission and do that duty for many years as if one day lives would depend on it.

"I know he died because he made the decision to go back inside after people who needed him," says Susan Rescorla. "He lived to help others, and there was no way he ever would have left that building until that duty was done and his mission was complete. He died doing that duty."

Tim Stackpole was a family man with a simple perspective on life. He believed in helping others with every fiber of his being, and he decided early on in his life that he wanted his job to be about that, too. Tim could have done a lot of different things for a living. His father was a pressman for the *New York Times,* and for a time Tim did consider a career in publishing. He started out studying business in college, and he could have made a run at the financial world after college too. But when he was twenty-one, he finally realized what it was he wanted to do for the rest of his life. He wanted to save lives as a fireman.

That's about the same time Tim met his future wife, Tara, through family friends in the neighborhood. But only fifteen, she was just a kid at the time. Tim thought of her like a little sister who he could joke around with. Their joking grew into a real friendship as Tara grew older, and when she turned twenty-one, they both suddenly realized there was something more to their relationship. A year later, Tim asked the woman of his dreams to marry him. The happy couple didn't waste any time filling the house with living proof of their love—five children, four boys and one darling little girl.

Tim grew up on the streets of Brooklyn. For his entire life, he went to the same church, hung out with the same friends, lived in the same neighborhood, and got up each morning with the same thing on his mind—he wanted to be a good son, a good friend, a good family man, and a good fireman.

Tim fared well with all those goals. He loved his wife and family with all his heart. He helped out at his church with retreats and charity work, plus he and Tara were pre-marriage counselors in their spare time. Living just a few blocks from his parents, he was always there for them to call on, and dinner at Mom and Dad's was frequent. Peaceful and forgiving by nature, Tim was always the one called on to patch up family problems or end an argument, and he always came to the rescue. As a fireman, Tim was one of New York's finest, saving hundreds of lives during his seventeen years on the job because that was his mission. It was his duty to save lives.

Tara couldn't have asked for a better husband. Tim worked hard, but he was always ready with a kind word or a hug when he came home. He worked a second job installing and fixing air conditioners to help out with the bills for the big family, but he always made time to sit and talk with his wife, to share his ideas and perceptions of the day, and to ask her what was on her mind.

That's exactly what he was doing one warm June day in 1998. He sat and had a cup of tea with Tara before heading off to fight a fire just like he'd done a thousand times before.

At 8:22 P.M. on June 5, 1998, Tim and his colleagues from Rescue Unit Two, known for their bravery and cool handling of hot fires, arrived at a small fire that had sprung up in some row houses in East New York. But what began as a minor mattress fire soon erupted into a five-alarm inferno, as the wood-frame structures went up like tinder. By the time Tim and his colleagues worked their way inside the buildings, they were staring at a catastrophe waiting to happen.

Within minutes, 225 fireman were on the scene. While other firefighters bravely fought the flames, Tim, the experienced veteran, hustled into the adjacent buildings to figure out where the fire would spread to next and find a way to stop it. He took a few rookies with him, but fearing the situation inside could be more dangerous than it looked, he told the rookies to wait as he made his way into one of the structures. Unbeknownst to Tim, while he was assessing the situation on the second floor, the fire had spread to the first floor beneath him. When a woman began screaming that her mother was trapped inside the building Tim was in, another team of firefighters rushed in to rescue her. Just as they burst into the building, the entire floor between the first and second stories gave way, sending Tim falling into a pit of fire and burying him, along with his fellow firemen who were searching on the floor below, under a ton of flaming debris.

The situation looked bleak. Some of his colleagues already lay dead beside him, while Tim lay helpless but alive under the inescapable pile of flames. His radio was beside him but he was unable to get to it, and he listened in agony to his fellow firefighters search for him in vain. He was incapable of directing them, or even letting them know he was still alive. Meanwhile, the flames were burning through his thick layers of protective garb. And now Tim Stackpole felt the full power of the fire for the first time. He realized he was going to be burned alive.

As the indescribable pain sent him into hysteria, he ripped off his oxygen mask and screamed, hoping someone would hear him. Even if they didn't, he thought, at least with his mask off he would pass out and die from smoke inhalation instead of being burned alive. But Tim refused to stop trying. He screamed out the Lord's Prayer, hoping that either God or his friends would take him out of that place soon.

Suddenly, he heard the lifesaving sound of his fellow fire-fighters as they stormed the room, dousing the flames and rescuing his charred body. Amazed that he was still alive, a friend handed him a string of rosary beads to give him hope while they rushed him to a nearby hospital. The doctors stabilized him before rushing him to the burn unit at Cornell Hospital in Manhattan. All the time, through the fire and through the pain, Tim remained conscious, fighting to live.

Meanwhile, his wife, Tara, was eating out with some friends when the fire department chaplain, who was a close friend of the family, tracked her down. He wanted to tell her the news personally before she heard about it on TV. Tara immediately rushed to her fallen husband's side.

As he lay in a hospital bed with almost half his body covered with third-degree burns, Tim's main concern was for those who didn't make it out. He thanked those who rescued him, and he told Tara how much he loved her and how proud he was to be a fireman. She comforted her husband and looked at him with hope and amazement. She fell in love with a hero so many years ago. And as scared as she was, she was proud of him.

But Tim was in bad shape. His legs were burned right through to the bone. Doctors were amazed he was still alive—and conscious to boot. But while they rushed to treat his serious and debilitating burns, another even more serious problem arose. When he removed his mask in the fire, the smoke had entered his lungs and caused serious damage. Within a few hours after arriving at the burn center, Tim stopped breathing and was placed on a respirator. Doctors feared the worst and induced a coma in order to prevent him from further causing himself pain or injury.

While her mother tended to the children at home, Tara stood by Tim's side day and night—hoping, praying, waiting, and watching through it all. As much as he was her hero, she was surely his, too. She tried hard to hold back her fears and tears as his condition worsened over the next few days. Although his burns began to respond to treatment, his lungs did not. The respirator kept him alive while doctors tried to figure out what was happening. They reduced his chances for survival to slim to none.

But Tara refused to believe any of it. She had lived more than half her life now with the man who made miracles happen all the time because of his love, and she knew he had one more miracle in him now. All she had to do was love him the way he loved her, their children, and everybody who ever came into contact with hero Tim Stackpole.

As sure as Tim's life was about giving, somebody up there felt the need to give Tim back to Tara. A few days later, his lungs suddenly began to respond to the antibiotics, rapidly improving enough to take him off the respirator. Doctors breathed a sigh of relief as Tim began breathing on his own. Tara broke down in tears of joy at her husband's side as he regained consciousness after coming out of the drug-induced coma. She hugged her husband so fiercely doctors warned her to be careful not to hurt him. Tim just smiled as if he always knew it would be okay.

But Tim was far from out of the woods. His legs were in bad shape. He would be lucky if he could ever live a normal life again.

But as soon as he could talk, Tim told his wife how much he wanted to get back to work. He was so grateful for those who saved him, and he wanted to get back in the field and help them. Some thought Tara should be upset with her husband for telling her he wanted to go back to work after what she'd been through, almost losing him and all. But Tara wasn't angry. How could she be? Tim was just being the hero he was, the hero she married, the man who always did his duty. He wasn't about to stop now.

Doctors pacified him at times. Other times they told him the honest truth, that he was lucky to be alive and that he might never walk again. And he would most certainly never fight a fire again. But every time they told him that, Tim stubbornly denied it. He would be able to walk again. He would be there for Tara and the children. And he would be a fireman again.

Two months later, Tim was wheeled out of the hospital. A line of firefighters dressed in full uniform saluted him as a hero. But Tim didn't feel like a hero, not yet. For him the heroes were those who saved him and those who stood by him. As the wheelchair made its way through the gauntlet of towering, steely eyed firefighters, all standing at attention honoring Tim, he suddenly stopped at the end of the line. Tim was sweating bullets as he struggled through the pain to triumphantly push himself up from his wheelchair and stand on his battered, bleeding limbs. With his wife and parents by his side, he stood for as long as it took to shake hands with every firefighter there. Then he asked everyone to pray for the firefighters who didn't make it, and he thanked his rescuers for saving his life and for reuniting him with his family. A limo sent by his brethren took Tim home with a fire engine escort, sirens blasting all the way, while firemen, neighbors, friends, and fans cheered him on. For blocks around his home neighbors saluted the hometown hero with red, white, and blue balloons, plus signs and banners to let him know they loved him for always doing his duty. Tim still didn't think he deserved such recognition.

At Mass that Sunday, parishioners applauded Tim's recovery and his return home. He thanked God and his family for his good fortune and for allowing him to serve. Everyone was grateful to have Tim alive.

For Tim, the easy part was over. He didn't feel like a hero for surviving. The only way he could earn that honor was to get back to work doing his duty. But doctors told him it was time for him to settle down at home with Tara and the kids. After bravely battling fires for all those years and narrowly escaping death, he certainly deserved it. But Tim had a different vision. Just as he proved the doctors wrong when they said he would never stand on his own two feet again, he was determined to prove he would fight fires once again.

Over the next few months and with a great deal of therapy, Tim made slow but steady progress. He knew in his heart that it was just a matter of time before he would be ready to start rehabilitating his legs and eventually go back to work. It was his duty, and Tara understood. He told her if he just accepted his condition and retired, he could never live with himself because there were people out there he was capable of saving. That was his mission, and he aimed to complete it.

The fight to rehabilitate himself was tough. Dozens of painful and dangerous surgeries and skin grafts would be necessary over the next several years if he wanted to try to get back his full mobility, plus he would have to deal with countless complications caused by infections. His legs were completely covered with the scars of his torturous experience, and his dream of walking again could only happen with years of therapy and hard work. It would all have been so much easier if he just sat back and collected his disability checks and let himself heal over the long haul. But that was unacceptable to Tim. He had a job to do.

Every day he pushed himself up onto his battered limbs and struggled to put one foot in front of the other while wracked with so much pain he frequently fell to the ground dizzy and nauseous in agony. But every day he would try again. With tiny victories, one step at a time, Tim did the work. By the end of his second year out of the hospital, Tim was walking on his own and ready to start strength-training.

Three years later, in March 2001, Tim returned to his job firefighting.

Refusing to take it easy at work, Tim was back up to full speed in weeks. And a few months later, on September 9, 2001, the fire department's Emerald Society presented Tim with its Man of the Year Award for his outstanding service to the community on and off the job.

Two days later, on September 11, 2001, Tim reported to work for the first time as a captain, a promotion that was well deserved. He wasn't supposed to go in that day, but he wanted to help out. He just didn't feel right about staying home right after receiving such an honor and a promotion. He reported to his precinct, which was also central headquarters for the FDNY, and went straight in to see the fire chief to confer on a few matters. That's when all hell broke loose in New York City as a commercial jetliner slammed into one of the towers of the World Trade Center.

Tim grabbed his gear and jumped into the chief's car. They rushed to the scene, along with every other rescue worker in the city. When they arrived a few minutes later, what they saw was worse than they ever could have imagined. Hundreds of fire-fighters were already scrambling to save as many lives as possible, but the destruction was so widespread that few knew where to start. Flames poured from the midsection of the tower, cutting off people at the top from rescue. Young rookies broke under the strain of such horrors, frozen in fear and confusion and not knowing how to help or what to do next. But Captain Stackpole, an experienced church counselor and a longtime trainer on the force, immediately began rallying the rookies with the help of an FDNY chaplain. Together they comforted them, shored up their confidence, and shook them from their shock. Tim reminded them that, first and foremost, their duty was to save lives.

Just then the second plane hit, and Tim ran inside the building to rescue those trapped in the suffocating smoke. Nobody knows for sure what happened to Captain Timothy Stackpole after that, except that his body was found lying at the base of Ground Zero where he made his last stand to do his duty and save lives. But Tim Stackpole is not a hero because of how he died or simply what he did in the last few minutes of his life. He's a hero because of how he *lived*. Tim Stackpole embodied every worthwhile reason why we should get up every day and go to work.

Tim's funeral was befitting of a head of state. The entire fire department, the fire department band, police officers, and even Mayor Rudolph Giuliani packed Brooklyn's Good Shepherd Church, where Tim went every Sunday as a child and where he married his wife. The mayor broke down crying as he spoke glowingly of the fallen fireman who believed so much in doing his duty that he spent three years fighting to earn the right to work again.

Tara says she misses Tim every single day, but she knows he did what he had to do. And in those dark or lonely moments when it gets too much to bear, she looks at her children and knows her husband instilled in them that same commitment to live a good life and to do their duty, whatever that might be.

"So many people didn't understand why my husband wanted to go back on the job after that terrible injury," says Tara. "But that was him. He lived to help people and to love people. He believed in doing his duty and never giving up on it. I can't fault him for that very thing I loved him for. Would I rather have him here with me today? Of course I would. But I know wherever Tim is he's happy now and he left an incredible legacy to our children to always do your duty with honor and love in your heart."

CHAPTER FOUR

◆ The Principle of Self-Respect

> *"To have that sense of one's intrinsic worth which constitutes self-respect is potentially to have everything: the ability to discriminate, to love and to remain indifferent. To lack it is to be locked within oneself, paradoxically incapable of either love or indifference."*
>
> —Joan Didion, *Slouching Towards Bethlehem*

Do you love yourself? I mean really and truly love yourself? Are you concerned enough about your personal well-being to protect your own self-interest?

This might seem like a strange topic for a book about heroism, but the truth is, if you don't respect yourself, you aren't capable of loving and respecting others enough to be anyone's hero. Few people realize just how easy it is to get caught up in a dangerous rut of self-abusive or self-destructive behavior. The result: great human pain and suffering for the whole of society.

Just look how this plays out in the many different aspects of your own life. Let's get personal here for just a minute. Have you ever been involved with someone who suffered from very low self-esteem? Was that person a kind and supportive source of love and kindness? Or, more often, was that person bitter, jealous, and possessive, suspecting the worst of you and abusing you in return for your affection? How many times have such people explained their difficult behavior to you by claiming it's the result of a bad past relationship experience or a bad up-bringing? What they are really saying is that something abusive happened to them that made them doubt their self-worth. That low self-image ultimately translates into a low image of humanity in general which results in abusive treatment of others.

Or consider disciplinary problems you might have with your children. How many times does the real cause of a behavior problem turn out to be something altogether different than you might think—peer pressure, bullying, or a perceived sense of physical, intellectual, or social inadequacies. Often, the rebellious child is actually suffering from feelings of worthlessness. Why do many children do drugs? Because they want to be liked, or they want to fit in. Why do they want so badly to be liked that they are willing to hurt themselves? Because they don't feel worthy of being liked for themselves.

Look at society as a whole, and you'll see much of the same pattern. Criminals and addicts were usually brought up being told they were only capable of the minimum in life and suffered from low opinions of themselves for years. That leads them to believe that limited lives are all they deserve—that they don't merit the fruits of an honest living. It's a vicious cycle of self-hate, self-hurt, and wasted lives.

In fact, so much hurtful or evil behavior in the world can be traced back to this lack of self-respect. Napoleon, Hitler, even serial killers like Charles Manson all struggled with bad self-images at young ages. Their insecurities and feelings of worthlessness translated into inferior perspectives on human worth in general. Obviously, a multitude of social and psychological forces are at work in such complex individuals, but underlying self-esteem is inarguably one of those major factors. Ultimately, having a low opinion of one's self and of others leads troubled individuals to practice abusive and destructive behavior.

What Is Self-Respect?

The starting point of this book—love—is, as expected, the starting point of this chapter on self-respect, too. Love for humanity must begin in the most basic and obvious place it can—within us in the form of deep and meaningful self-respect. All the self-sacrifice and well-intentioned giving in the world cannot work if, in your heart, you believe you are worthless. If that's the case, then anything that comes from you will also be worthless. Every major religion in the world promotes the concept of self-respect as the basic starting point to a divine life, yet it is consistently the most overlooked tenet of living a life of love for others.

So how do you know you are worthy in the first place? You are worthy because humanity itself has worth. We have all been endowed by God with divinity. But even if you remove God from the equation, one can still conclude that we are all worthwhile based on simple humanism. In other words, as a society we have decided to try and prosper; therefore, our common goal is for the betterment of mankind. We have decided as a society that man is worthwhile. If mankind has worth, each one of us is inherently valuable. That means respecting ourselves and others is the only logical way to live.

So empowering ourselves to be strong, confident, healthy, and joyous in our hearts and heads should be our goal. A simpler way of saying this is simply that taking care of ourselves makes it easier for us to take care of others. Then one can go out and apply all the other principles of this book in their interactions with others and live the life of a hero.

How Can I Bring a Sense of Self-Respect into My Life?

Before we can accomplish this goal of self-respect, it's crucial to realize that most people don't live in a manner that is really in their best self-interest at all, even though they might think they do. Instead, they frequently act to damage themselves either physically, mentally, or spiritually because they feel, either consciously or subconsciously, that they are worthless. Ultimately, this inability or refusal to care for ourselves leads us to hurting others. Inevitably, we will all fall prey to this behavior from time to time, but if we know how to spot it when it creeps into our lives we can at least try to stop it.

But self-respect does not mean self-indulgence. Before you embark on some whirlwind, decadent pleasure-quest in a misdirected attempt to "love your fellow man," remember this: Self-respect does not promote simple self-gratification. Rather, the route to self-respect is through a long-term commitment to enduring human fulfillment and success.

For instance, people smoke for some temporary or immediate high or pleasure, even though they know it will perhaps kill them eventually or saddle them with extraordinary long-term illnesses. This is obviously not self-serving in the long run, either to the smoker, his loved ones, or the rest of society. Although the smoker might wrongly believe he or she is acting in his own best self-interest by doing what he or she wishes, they are actually acting against their own best self-interest in the end and hurting society at the same time. All this damage to others stems from one's inability to do what is ultimately best for oneself.

Consider just about any of the social ills. In the end, it is a deep-felt lack of self-interest that promotes these obviously self-abusive behaviors and eventually socially destructive behaviors. A thief steals because he desires money, but in the long run such a lifestyle is not at all in his own best self-interest, because it inevitably leads to alienation, incarceration, and possibly even premature death. The same can be said for any addictive behavior such as drugs, alcohol, gambling, etc. Just about any criminal behavior can be explained as such.

But on the other hand, when people do respect their long-term best self-interest, it usually translates into an overall benefit for humanity and society. So to love oneself leads to loving others because of a love for humanity. That love for humanity then leads back to reinforce one's love for oneself. This circular cycle of love gets stronger with every round it completes.

Specifically, how do we learn how to respect ourselves? To sincerely respect yourself means taking care of your long-term needs. That means first of all maintaining your mental, physical, and spiritual health. If you know something is harmful, refrain or attempt to diminish that activity or desire as much as possible. If you know an activity is constructive, pursue it. In the simplest of terms, this means eating healthful foods, fueling your mind with useful information, and promoting your spirit with uplifting and positive experiences and people. But there are reams of books and guides that can help you in this regard, so we won't even begin to go into that. What's important for the sake of this book is the understanding that self-respect should be the goal and how you absolutely *cannot* love others without first taking care of yourself.

Once an individual has mastered the challenges of respecting oneself, respecting others becomes the natural next step. As proof of this, witness all the addicts and criminals who, after reforming their lives, turn around and throw themselves headfirst into helping others. Once they have realized the ability to respect the humanity in themselves, they begin to have a natural desire to respect that same humanity when they see it in others.

Cheryl Sesnon's inspiring story shows how one woman changed her own world, then the worlds of many others, to make life more meaningful for all. Her road of self-discovery to eventual self-respect took many twists and turns. Some of those lead her precariously close to ending her life. But in the end, she discovered the secret to self-respect was not achieving greatness, pleasure, or material gain. In fact, it wasn't the achievement of anything; rather, it was appreciation for what she already had.

ADDICTED TO LOVE

Moving all over the world with a military family might sound fun and exciting, but for Cheryl Sesnon it was a nightmare. The constant relocation made it even harder for the insecure girl to fit in anywhere. As she struggled to be happy and healthy in a family already plagued with depression and other mental health problems, it was only a matter of time before she came face to face with her own deadly demons and her lifelong struggle to love herself.

By the time she was thirteen years old, Cheryl was using drugs regularly. Her family was stationed in Germany, and she saw drugs as a way to make friends quickly and be accepted by her peers. "I was willing to do just about anything to be liked back then," admits Cheryl. "Moving all the time and starting over again in each new place made me feel so insecure. So when some of the other kids pulled out some hash in the bathroom, I did it. It wasn't really about the drugs; it was about proving I was worth something to someone."

Cheryl's drug abuse was only one symptom of her tremendous lack of self-respect and self-esteem. Alcoholism and a series of abusive relationships soon followed. By the time she was sixteen years old, Cheryl was staying out until the wee hours of the morning, partying and using drugs and alcohol. When she came home one night too drunk to walk, her mom kicked her out of the house.

"Instead of waking me up to the fact that I had a problem that I needed to deal with, that just further assured me that I was worthless and that the world was a horrible place," says Cheryl. "I basically became clinically depressed after that." The rejection from her mother convinced Cheryl that there was no love in the world, even from her own family. "My view of life was that it was a terrible and painful experience. Whenever I saw someone who was happy," remembers Cheryl, "I used to think they were just crazy or stupid."

Soon after that, Cheryl found work as a bartender, a job that allowed her to get drunk every night and live a wayward lifestyle without really arousing much suspicion that there was anything wrong with her. "Everybody I worked with was always getting drunk and doing drugs anyway, so I fit right in," she recalls. "I just kept up the same self-abusive habits and thought I was fine." But inside Cheryl was miserable, and her world was getting darker and darker with each passing day.

Again looking for the outward approval and validation she was lacking within, she started dating her manager, a dashing man almost a decade older than herself. Together the two lived life like rock stars—Cheryl spent her days and nights boozing it up, doing drugs, and partying all night long after work almost every day of the week. "I was so young and afraid, and he was the ultimate image of success and power," remembers Cheryl.

Although Cheryl was racing down the road to ruin, it was the first time in her life the insecure teenager felt she was important. "It didn't matter that his life was falling apart because of his addictions," says Cheryl. "All I saw was that this authority figure wanted me, which meant I must be important. Everybody wanted to be around him, and I felt special because he picked me—I felt like somebody."

But the hard-living crowd and the fast-lane lifestyle were starting to take a toll on Cheryl. Before long, she was hooked on coke and her life was spiraling further and further out of control. "It seemed like the harder and harder I tried to be liked, the less and less I liked myself," remembers Cheryl. At an all-time low, she didn't know how to turn it all around. "I just figured that's life, you know," says Cheryl. "I thought the world was just a horrible place, and I couldn't understand how anybody was ever happy to be alive. No matter what I did, I couldn't stop seeing the world that way."

Having lost all concern for her own well-being by that point, it was actually her love for her boyfriend that inspired Cheryl to take the first step toward realizing there was something wrong with the way she was living. She watched him struggling with his own excesses, and she credits that for being her first eye-opening experience. "He was killing himself with booze and drugs," remembers Cheryl. "I knew it was just a matter of time before he was dead, and I couldn't bear the thought of watching the man I cared for die like that."

Cheryl finally left her boyfriend for good. But she still struggled with the same issues of self-worth, and she wound up right back in other doomed relationships for the next several years, eventually hooking up with an emotionally abusive man who led her to seek relief in antidepressives and Valium. Unable to help herself, she tried to help others instead. One night she found herself with a gun pointed at her head, held captive by a friend's obsessed boyfriend after she warned her to stop seeing the crazed man. "I thought for sure I was going to die," remembers Cheryl. "When he finally let me go, I couldn't even believe I was alive. But what was strange was that for the first time I remember feeling like if I died, it wouldn't have been a big deal. That's how depressed I was."

Although Cheryl made it through that scrape, it was only a temporary reprieve. The problems and pains of living with such overbearing feelings of worthlessness only grew worse each year. She knew something was wrong, but she didn't know what—and more important, she didn't believe her problems would ever allow her to be happy.

By the time she was twenty-five years old, her suffering and self-hatred had finally reached such a boiling point that she decided she just couldn't take it anymore. She was ready to call it quits and end her life.

One evening Cheryl undressed, got into the bathtub, and slowly slashed both her wrists with a razor. "I sat there under the warm water and just let them bleed," reveals Cheryl. "I figured no more pain, no more sadness. It was all going to finally be over, and I could leave this horrible world."

But as Cheryl sat in the tub watching the life gush out of her, suddenly it occurred to her that maybe she was missing something. Could there be something worth living for inside her after all? Was she looking at life all wrong? Maybe there really was something worthwhile about life and about people, and ultimately something good inside her. "I can't really explain it," says Cheryl, "but somehow, as I thought about losing everything, I realized that I *did* have something to lose. My life meant something." She thought again about all those happy, crazy, and stupid people out there she always criticized. Did they know something she didn't? Maybe she could learn something from them. "I didn't quite know what that was yet," says Cheryl, "but at least I was ready to find out."

Weak from the loss of blood, Cheryl struggled to bandage her wrists well enough to slow the bleeding so she could rush herself to the hospital before she lost consciousness. She arrived just in the nick of time, and doctors saved her life.

The next day she realized she was going to have to find a new way of looking at the world and herself or she was going to wind up right back in that bathtub ready to die again. "I had to erase everything I thought I knew and start over," explains Cheryl. "I realized a few days later what my problem was. I thought everything about life was bad—men were pigs, the world was a terrible place, people were all liars and cheats.

* COMPARE TO ALBERT CAMUS, ERIC HOFFER AND AUGUSTEN BURROUGHS

Everyone was worthless including me. There was nothing but misery, hatred, and hurt in my version of the world. The best you could do was to bear the pain." If she wanted to go on living, she knew she would need to admit to herself that the way she saw the world was not reality but only her own self-inflicted nightmare—one that she could awaken from.

Cheryl decided to start fresh by looking at people who were successful and happy and emulating how they lived. "I knew the way I looked at life wasn't working," says Cheryl, "so I realized I had to look to people whose lives *were* working for guidance. That was only logical. As soon as I really started looking at those people's lives, I realized there were people in the world who really were happy, even though they weren't perfect or didn't fit into what somebody else thought they should be. I didn't understand exactly how those people thought about life yet, but I could try to copy their behavior patterns and at least get my life together."

One of the first things she noticed was that those happy people filled their lives with the opportunities to love and to be loved, and they always had a positive attitude toward people and situations in general. "The negativity was the hardest thing for me to get rid of," explains Cheryl, "but I saw time and time again how people who were happy saw the best in other people they interacted with every day, and in themselves, too. They believed that life was great because they could help others and spread joy."

Cheryl soon realized that the greatest difference between her

72

and happy people was that every time something went wrong in her life, she used it as an excuse to condemn herself and a reason to hate humanity and life in general. "I realized that these healthy and happy people were content in spite of their problems," says Cheryl. "They just had a strategy for dealing with life and all those problems that didn't include beating themselves or anybody else up in the process. They respected themselves and respected others no matter what."

As Cheryl's self-perception and her image of people on the whole improved, so did her life. Soon she was making a good living as a finance person for a car dealership, making new friends and enjoying a more stable and sustainable life. But as she began to love her life, herself, and others, she began to feel a natural desire to express that new positive attitude on the job. And that meant finding a job she could be proud of. "I wanted to grow in my work, too," says Cheryl. "I was always very fair with people, and the car business wasn't really known for integrity and respect. I thought I could maybe make the business better if I worked my way up the ladder. But my boss told me flat out that a woman would never rise any higher in that industry than I was." The old Cheryl might have been shattered by such rejection, but the new, empowered Cheryl walked out the door and went to work for a female-owned dealership where she found great success by respecting her customers.

Now in a better place, emotionally and mentally, Cheryl finally met and married a respectful man, and the couple had a child. The two started a cake catering company and seemed poised for great success, but Cheryl soon found herself becoming co-dependent, and it was threatening her newfound self-esteem. "I didn't realize that I was going right back to where I was before in some ways needing someone else to make me feel worthwhile," says Cheryl. "Then it hit me that the only way to really respect yourself is to take ownership of your life."

While continuing to work with her husband, Cheryl tried harder and harder to be independent. But as she grew out of needing her husband's approval and became very successful at running the company, the marriage began to suffer. "I think he was very unhappy and bitter when he realized that I didn't need him like a drug anymore," explains Cheryl. "I was evolving, and he wanted to stay in the same place."

Meanwhile, the company was booming. Cheryl was a workhorse on the job, and her newfound happiness and positive perspective on life translated into a dynamic presence with customers.

But there was one more step she needed to take on her road to happiness, and her employees gave her the final shove. "They all came to me together and told me that they didn't want to work for me anymore," reveals Cheryl. "They said that all I ever did was work, but that I never asked them about their lives or told them about mine. They wanted me to respect them as people, not just employees."

For the next week, Cheryl hid from her employees, feeling guilty and confused. "I was going right back into that cycle of feeling worthless again," admits Cheryl. But she finally realized it was time for her to do more than just copy the way happy people acted. It was time for her to allow herself to *be* a happy person and share that happiness with everyone in her life, not just her customers. "I made a commitment right then and there to always appreciate and respect people just as I had learned to respect myself, and let them know how I felt," says Cheryl. "It totally changed my life when I realized that was the whole point of life."

She started by making the time to talk to her employees more, not just about work, but also about life and their feelings. That eventually evolved into changing the way she spoke, learning how to speak from her head and her heart at the same time. "It's not only important what you say, but how you say it, too—being sensitive to another person's feelings," explains Cheryl. "It's not just about the results, it's also about how you get there and how you make people feel along the way." As Cheryl began to focus on the means and not just the end result in life, she began to feel happier and more content than she had ever felt. "I finally truly loved myself and loved others. It was a total transformation from the way I had looked at life for so many years. Now I knew why all those people who I thought were so stupid were smiling. It didn't matter if there were problems in my life or if people who worked for me weren't perfect or I wasn't perfect as long as we all loved ourselves and each other and worked hard to be all that we could be. It was all about respect."

The happier Cheryl became, the harder she worked at helping others. Although her marriage ultimately ended, the couple remained friends and supportive parents of their child. Cheryl went to culinary school and got a degree. While still running the cake business, she began volunteering for a social services program that brought meals to the needy. At first she helped out by sharing recipes and pitching in with some of the cooking. But soon she was getting involved in the nitty gritty of the operation. "I really wanted to help these people in whatever way I could, and to share that great feeling of inner worth," remembers Cheryl. "Plus it was in an area where I could really contribute because of my hospitality background, so I just dove right in."

When Cheryl found out the operation was having trouble raising money, she was more than happy to step in as a fundraiser, putting her years of experience as a business owner to work for them. Her efforts gave the program a much-needed monetary boost, and her hardworking attitude toward helping others made her shine to the board members. Less than a year later, she was asked to become a boardmember herself. Not long after that, when the charity's acting director was fired, Cheryl was asked to help look for a replacement. After months of fruitless searching, Cheryl decided she would step up to the challenge herself. "I never even thought about actually making this my job when I started helping out," says Cheryl, "but I realized I had the qualifications and they couldn't find anybody to run the place, so it seemed like the right thing for me to do."

Cheryl put her combination of hospitality skills, business

savvy, and heartfelt devotion to helping people to work and turned the struggling operation around in a heartbeat. Then just a month after being on the job, she saw an opportunity to turn the organization in a different direction by applying what she had learned from her own lifelong struggle. Many of the organization's clients as well as workers were homeless people who couldn't hold down a job because they were suffering from the same self-esteem problems she had suffered for so many years. Over a lifetime, their feelings of worthlessness prevented them from developing the needed skills and positive attitude toward life necessary for success at any level. "It was a very noble effort to feed the homeless, but the organization was so upside down and disorganized that there wasn't much good being done," remembers Cheryl. "And so many of those people really needed a job more than food." She decided to transform the meals program into a complete life-skills program aimed at helping the homeless find employment and start over with a second chance at success. "I thought why not teach them what I had learned and then instead of just getting a meal or two from us they can learn how to have a lifetime of meals, and so much more."

What began as that simple idea, Cheryl soon learned was exactly what her entire life of struggle had prepared her perfectly to do. Most of the people on the street were suffering from the same ills that she had fought her whole life, like substance abuse and a bad attitude. Their low self-esteem constantly sent them into self-destructive behavioral patterns, which ultimately resulted in them seeing the world as a terrible and painful place. "If I could simply teach them what I had come to understand—that life was not about being perfect or beating yourself up for not being good enough," says Cheryl. "Then maybe they could stop looking at themselves as failures and get onboard in life."

Cheryl formulated a plan for teaching people how to respect themselves and others, implanting in them the desire and ability to be a contributing member of society. With the help of a corporate counselor, she created a sixteen-week program she named Fare Start. The intensive job-training program prepares homeless people for jobs in the food-service industry. There, the homeless learn everything from how to fill out a job application to how to speak to an employer. But most important, they learn how to get along with others at work and how to feel good about what you do. "If you shift your perspective to valuing yourself and others instead of devaluing or criticizing yourself and others, suddenly your eyes open to a whole new perspective on happiness and success," says Cheryl.

Its first year up and running, Fare Start graduated nine people. Since then, there have been almost a thousand. More than 90 percent of them get and hold down jobs, turning a life on the streets into a life back on their feet. "That's about four times the national average of homeless people who ever get off the streets," says Cheryl proudly. But what really moves Cheryl is that many of the people her program has helped were truly at the end of their rope when they came to Fare Start. "I know just how those people feel, because it's how I used to feel," says

Cheryl. "The loneliness, sadness, and self-hatred make you think death is a welcome alternative. But it's a terrible illusion. Now when I look at the world and myself, all I see is happiness and the incredible power of people to make great things happen."

CHAPTER FIVE

◆ The Principle of Faith

"The faith that stands on authority is not faith."

—Ralph Waldo Emerson

Once upon a time, there was a man who refused to believe in anything but himself. He was so faithless, he didn't trust a single person. He refused to believe in God, in love, in family, or even in real and genuine friendship, claiming that all these things were just foolish delusions that weak people use as crutches. He suggested that we strive to be a race of superbeings, creatures who don't need anyone but ourselves to survive. "Faith is not wanting to know the truth," he proclaimed obstinately.

That man was Friedrich Nietzsche, the famous philosopher whose refusal to believe in anyone or anything but himself and his work sucked him into a lifelong spiral of despair. He eventually went insane, dying from the complications of syphilis. But right before his unceremonious death, his final, dismal words were recorded for posterity. Forty years later, Nietzsche's last words were used by Adolf Hitler to justify his attempts at creating a super race of "superior beings" by means of genocide. Death is the only thing you reap when you have no faith in life.

"I believe in you," is just about the most powerful phrase anybody can say. It immediately changes the person who says it and the person it is said to into strong and powerful allies, two people who are exponentially stronger together than apart. It develops a bond between those individuals that makes anything possible, and it provides for a direct love line between those two human beings who become each other's heroes.

Every day, all over the world, people who believe in each other make miracles happen. How many times have you heard some inventor or person who did something extraordinary talk about how they could not have done it without that special person, whomever it was behind them who believed in them the whole way through? Isn't it simply amazing what that faith and trust make possible?

Did you ever hear that old saying "love is blind"? It really should be that love is faith, because love cannot be proven. When you love somebody, yes, it's partly because of the wonderful loving things they do and the harmful things they don't do. Add that to the way they look, act, sound, and smell, plus all kinds of other practical considerations, and you have all the essential building blocks of romantic love. But in the final analysis, love is a choice you make to trust someone with your heart, soul, and life. It's a decision to believe someone is the one for

you, even though there is no absolutely verifiable way of proving it. It's the commitment to believe in someone, even though
you have absolutely no assurances they will love you back the
way they promise to. In the end, love is all about trust and a leap
of faith. And without leaping, it's impossible to fall into love—
with a person, with the world, or with God.

I ✶ love defined

The love of humanity, the true route to happiness and heroism, is about faith in the many different people and experiences—
God, family, friends, country, community, and mankind
overall—all of which are part of the human event.

We have come to live in a very empirical age. Rather than
trusting our spouses, we hire detectives to spy on them. We
check on the sex of our children before they are born. We plan
vacations down to the minute like business trips, because we are
afraid to leave anything to chance. We say it's too hard to believe
in God because we can't see him. Deals are never done with a
handshake anymore but rather with an iron-clad contract.

Some of these tools of empiricism are worthwhile, even necessary. And I'm certainly not suggesting that people all over the
world jump willy-nilly in to marriages with people they hardly
know. But the exact opposite of that isn't a good idea, either.
The complete absence of faith in life is despair. Without faith,
love becomes impossible. And because the whole point of existence is love, a life without faith means a life without meaning
or joy, doomed to desolation.

What Is Faith?

◈ *The opposite of desolation is faith, the beautiful*
beacon of hopeful confidence we have in each other and
in life. Those who live with this spirit of cautious surprise look,
learn, and study, but eventually they dive into life. It's there that
they find the reason for living—love, and to believe in those
who choose to love us.

At its heart, faith is the commitment and desire to believe in
someone. It can be partially based on some element of observa-
tion of past occurrences or current facts, but it is finally a trust.
Eventually, every relationship you have in life, whether at work,
at home, or out on the street, requires a certain degree of faith.
Without faith in our parents, we would never let them care for
us. Without faith in our lovers, we would never tell them our
deepest secrets and show them our true inner selves, making in-
timacy possible. Without faith in our colleagues, we would never
work together. Finally, without faith in mankind, we would be
afraid to step foot on the street for fear of being killed or as-
saulted. If the human element of faith disappeared tomorrow,
civilization as we understand it would cease to exist.

With faith in each other, it's possible for us all to be connected in our efforts. It makes teamwork and partnering possible, thus allowing us to reap the reward of cooperation. It
allows us to become a strong, unified community, country, and
world. It allows for the separation and division of labor in so-

[handwritten margin note: ✻ THIS IS WARREN CHRISTOPHER'S POINT IN "A SHARED MOMENT OF TRUST."]

ciety. We don't all have to be doctors, lawyers, farmers, and engineers. We can depend on others to do their jobs while we do ours. We have faith that the doctor down the street will take care of us when we are sick, the lawyer will protect us in legal matters, and the farmer will feed us so we don't all have to grow our own food. We have faith that the driver next to us will obey traffic laws and stop at red lights, so we don't have to stop ourselves at every green light in fear that we will be killed entering the intersection. We trust that the government will protect us from foreign foes. We believe our tax money will be spent wisely and honestly. We go to work and trust that our employers will pay us two weeks later, which enables them to provide services for which others will pay them. Our entire economic system works, and modern society is made possible by faith.

How Can I Bring Faith into My Life?

◈ *We all possess faith, and to a rather extraordinary* degree. But when times are tough, or when we have been hurt by others, or maybe even just because we were never taught to trust as a child, sometimes some of us lose confidence in our ability to have faith. It is very important to society that these individuals be healed and their trust in mankind and society be restored. We can't just let such people linger in their faithlessness, because a faithless person is that much more likely to be unfaithful to others. Those who don't expect others to be true are so often convinced that others are betraying them that they see no reason why they shouldn't betray others in return. This cycle of distrust and betrayal once again threatens to destroy society if unchecked.

Heroes of faith come in many forms, and there are many ways we can heroically have faith. There are those whose belief in mankind inspires them to go out and give their hearts and souls to trusting and helping strangers on the street everyday. There are those whose extreme faith in family allows them to stand behind troubled loved ones when the rest of the world deserts them. There are hero friends who stick by you through thick and thin. There are bosses who take chances on employees whose past might be a little less than perfect. There are heroes in the criminal justice system whose faith in humanity allows them to work to rehabilitate prisoners on parole, confident that they will go forth and change their ways. The confidence in our fellow human beings that these heroes exhibit reach beyond explanation at times to another inexplicable result—the incredible, powerful, redemption of an individual previously thought lost in a world of their past mistakes or their own mistrust. And that is the simple but sometimes hard to accomplish single most important secret to having faith in our own lives. We must be willing to accept and defend the belief that all human beings are innately worthy of our trust and our faith. That is a far different perspective than the media espoused common cynicism that inspires us to trust no one.

But of all those forms of faith and trust, probably the most powerful and awe-inspiring of them all is the trust that develops in matrimony. When two strange hearts who never knew each other before come together to have total faith and trust in the other and to act in loyal accordance with that faith, it is a miraculous event that creates an unbreakable bond that nothing outside their relationship can truly threaten. That is the secret behind the miraculous and heartwarming story of John and Leslie Wilson.

HOW CAN I KNOW? } *John & Leslie Wilson — Marital Faith*

Leslie never trusted anyone her whole life, at least not after her mother abandoned her when she was seven, leaving the lost little girl with a father who didn't really know how to take care of her or even himself.

Growing up almost entirely on her own, she was living on the streets of San Francisco by the time she was fifteen years old and getting into one scrape after another. It was then that she adopted the motto she would live by for many years to come—trust no one and no one gets hurt! "My dad always used to say that you should trust people as far as you could throw them," says Leslie. "Well, I'm only five feet tall and weigh about a hundred pounds, so that's not very far."

For Leslie, believing in anyone or anything was hazardous to her health. She wanted one thing in life and that was to make it on her own. Friends were just people to hit the clubs with after work. Boyfriends were just people who could buy her time with gifts or dinners, and as for anything as meaningful as having a family one day, she didn't even think twice about it. "Attachments were for losers," says Leslie. "The second you depend on someone they will leave you. It was human nature as far as I thought. They are always trying to make you depend on them so they can get stuff from you. Then when they are done using you, they leave you flat. So why not just realize from the beginning that people are just out to use each other? Then you get what you want and I can get what I want."

It all made perfect sense to Leslie, and she went about living her less-than-inspired life true to form. The petite and perky blond with the piercing blue eyes was quite a hit when she found her calling as an exotic dancer. It was a job that paid well and fit perfectly into Leslie's cold and skeptical view of the world. "I knew what the men wanted," says Leslie, "and they knew what I wanted. Nobody got hurt because the transactions were all done in cash." She bared her body as a stripper for almost a decade, burying her heart as she mined men for money and nothing more. She hung out with a very wealthy but dishonest lot of people, and she did some very unsavory things to get what she wanted. She sold her body, stole, smuggled drugs, and even made a name for herself as a pornographic film star.

But it wasn't long before Leslie's wayward lifestyle got the better of her, landing her in a jail cell by the time she was twenty-three years old. "That was the lowest point of my life," says Leslie. A crooked lawyer got her off the hook in exchange for a few favors, but it was the first time Leslie had ever been behind bars, and she promised herself it would be the last. "The crazy part is that I wasn't as upset about being in jail as I was about needing to trust this lawyer to get me out. That part killed me."

Leslie pulled herself together and eventually got out of the seedy world of strip clubs and sex, saving up her cash and studying to get her real estate license. With California land values in nearby Silicon Valley skyrocketing, Leslie was in the right place at the right time. She moved houses the same way she moved people in and out of her life—quickly and without emotion. She knew what she wanted out of a house—money—and she gave it whatever it took to get it. Says Leslie, "It was the perfect job for me, because I didn't have to work with anyone else or depend on anyone to get money."

She put her past life behind her, changing her hair color, the way she dressed, and even going so far as legally changing her name. She was so ashamed that she never told a soul about her background, pretending she was an Army brat whose parents moved her around Europe until she came back to the States and started selling real estate. But her deep, dark secret would make it impossible for her to trust anyone, even the men she dated.

By the time she was twenty-six, Leslie was raking in a six-figure income. She was on top of the world, and she did it all by herself. She had everything she needed, and anything else she could buy. "The most important thing in the world for me was financial security," says Leslie. "If I had that, I figured nobody could ever hurt me. I used to date men to get that, but now I had it myself. I figured, what do I even need men for?—unless they could help me sell a house, because that was as good as money in the bank."

Her shallow and loveless life continued that way for several years, but everything changed when she met John, a young lawyer who seemed to have it all himself. He grew up with all the privileges of being from a wealthy New England family. He had heaps of cash, a nice house, and a luxurious car, and the six-foot-two former college basketball player was a hunk of a man to boot. But there was something different about John, something beyond his wealth that attracted Leslie to him. Even though he was well off, John wasn't like most of the other rich men Leslie had known. Although he appreciated nice dinners and nice cars, he didn't seem to need them. What he valued most was love. In fact, he spent every weekend volunteering his time to help underprivileged children at dozens of different agencies in the city, and he gave away much of his money to help with the programs.

John and Leslie met in the summer of 1986, and over the next three months, he fell head over heels in love with her. And although she didn't realize it yet, she was falling in love with him, too. "I wasn't in the habit of letting a man sweep me off my feet," says Leslie, "but there was something about John that got me going."

But loving somebody didn't really fit into Leslie's version of success. So as soon as she realized she was getting hooked, she started to pull away, leaving John hurt and confused. "We did

everything together, went everywhere, and talked about everything under the sun that first couple of months," remembers
Leslie. "But he was being honest with me, and I was just telling
him what I thought he wanted to hear. I didn't think I could
trust him with who I really was and the things I had done." But
for the first time in her life, Leslie actually wanted to believe in
a man. "The fact that I couldn't do it made me angry, and I took
out that anger on him."

The couple dated on and off again for the next year, breaking up every time Leslie started to get scared and getting together again every time John wooed her back. But incredibly,
after all that time, Leslie was still so afraid to confide in John
that she wouldn't even let him into her apartment because she
was terrified he'd find out something about her she didn't
want him to know. "It was totally irrational fear," admits Leslie.
"I made up all these reasons in my head why I needed to be
afraid of trusting him." But as John grew deeper and deeper in
love, Leslie grew only more frustrated by her inability to level
with him about her past. She found herself making up more
and more stories to cover her web of lies. "I never cheated on
him physically when we were together, but I was unfaithful in
my heart because I refused to trust him," says Leslie. "I never
believed in us. It was just too hard. I didn't have any role mod-
els for that. Nobody I ever knew trusted anyone and had it
work out."

As much as Leslie loved John, she couldn't give him what she
knew he wanted. And the more he trusted her with his heart,

the harder it was for her to keep seeing him. She decided to finally tell him it was over, leaving a heartless phone message on his answering machine then leaving town for the weekend before he got a chance to get back to her.

John was devastated. Even though Leslie was having trouble committing to loving him, he was sure beyond a shadow of a doubt of his love for her. When he got home from the office and heard the awful message, he immediately called her back and left a message of his own of two simple questions. "He said, 'Do you love me?' " recalls Leslie, " 'and if you do, will you marry me?' Men told me they loved me before. Heck, they even asked me to marry them. But nobody ever asked me if I loved them. I did love John, but I was afraid to admit it."

After Leslie returned home from her trip and listened to the startling phone message, she immediately picked up the phone and called John. She told him she loved him, but she wouldn't marry him, and she didn't want to see him for a while. Then she abruptly hung up the phone.

John respected her wishes, and he didn't call her back, figuring the ball was now in her court. "I really loved her," explains John, "but she just wasn't ready. Sometimes the best way to love someone is to leave them alone and trust that they'll come to you when the time is right." Meanwhile, the stress of it all was taking its toll on him. Plus life at the office was more demanding than ever. John began to have horrible migraines and wasn't sleeping well. He was growing tired of his fifteen-hour workdays, and he was considering taking on a partner. He thought about calling Leslie after a few days to tell her how much he loved her, but at the last minute he hung up the phone. "I didn't want her coming back to me because I chased her down," explains John. He hoped she would call soon, but after several weeks went by without hearing from her he began to think she might never call him again. Still, he had hope that she would come to her senses on her own. "I was pulling my hair out wanting to call her," says John, "but I needed to have faith that when she was ready she would call me. That was the only way it was ever going to work. She had to make the decision to trust me and believe in us. I couldn't just go running after her trying to force her into it."

Leslie was dealing with issues of her own at the time. She was heartbroken over her inability to commit to John, but she didn't know how to shake her fear. All of a sudden the whole game had changed. Although she had spent a lifetime learning to distrust everyone, now the most important person in her life was asking her to do the exact opposite. "I knew in my head that if I loved him, I had to stop all this nonsense and just trust him," explains Leslie, "but I couldn't." She was still afraid, and absurd fears kept running through her mind. What if she told him all about her and he didn't want her after that? Or even worse, what if he told others about her past and ruined her life? Before long the whole city would know, ruining her reputation and her business. "I really was thinking those crazy things," admits Leslie. "Here was the most wonderful and loving man I had ever known and I was worrying about him using information to

double-cross me. It was all just a great way of me making ex-
cuses for not wanting to trust anybody."

Although she knew in her heart that she loved John, she
could not bring herself to risk it all and tell him everything
about her. Once he knew about her he might leave her anyway,
then she would have nothing.

John was taking it all as best as he could, working hard and
keeping up with all of his responsibilities at the office while trying to keep his mind off Leslie. But without Leslie in his life,
work just seemed to be less and less meaningful. "Money has
never really been where it is for me," says John. "I would have
given it all up in a heartbeat if she said she would marry me."
He was getting ready to sign some preliminary papers with his
prospective new partner over breakfast a few weeks later when
who should he see walk in but Leslie. "I got this lump in my
throat the second I saw her," says John. "I still loved her with all
my heart." But John wasn't going to get all gushy in the middle
of business, plus he was still waiting for Leslie to make her decision. John politely said hello and introduced his prospective
partner, explaining that he was going to be taking on some of
his cases. Keeping things very casual, he was stunned when
Leslie became so agitated she suddenly excused herself and ran
off. "I knew things were a little awkward between us, but she
looked like she'd seen a ghost or something," remembers John.
"I couldn't figure out what happened."

What John couldn't have known is that Leslie had seen a
ghost—or at least a ghost from her past. Unbeknownst to John,

the man he introduced to Leslie, the man he was thinking of turning over his financial future to, was a man from Leslie's "past life"—the man who she went to jail because of, the man who got her out in exchange for her duplicity. His ties to organized crime ran deep, and it wasn't unusual for his business acquaintances to wind up dead or missing. "I will never forget that man for as long as I live," says Leslie. "He did some very bad things to a lot of people. But he always had a way of getting into high-class circles and taking people's money but coming out squeaky-clean himself. I was terrified for John."

Obviously, Leslie's new look and her new name hid her true identity, but he looked exactly the same. When John said this was a man he was thinking of getting involved in a business deal with, it sent chills down Leslie's spine. Now her entire world was suddenly turned upside down. John's life and livelihood were in her hands. She ran home scared and confused about what to do.

"I was not at all prepared to deal with any of this," says Leslie. "How could anyone be ready for that?" Leslie was still terrified of telling John about her past, but now it was more than just her personal fears that she had to think of. He had trusted her with his heart, and she threw it back in his face. But now the stakes were higher. "It was pretty easy to see that I was going to have to trust him in order to help him," says Leslie. "There was no other way, because how could I possibly explain the whole situation to him without divulging how I knew? The only other choice was to let him get hurt. I loved him too much to let that happen."

Fearing something terrible might happen before she had a chance to warn him, she called him and asked to come over that night. John was surprised, but happy to hear her voice. Two hours later, Leslie showed up at his door, and she brought her whole life with her. She was ready to do what she had never done before—trust a man and to have faith that their relationship was everything she felt in her heart. "It was terrifying," says Leslie. "I didn't want to get hurt, and everything I valued up until that point was on the line. I had to believe that he wouldn't take it all away from me. But his life was a whole lot more important than all that." She broke down in tears right there and told him everything about her. "I just couldn't help myself all of a sudden," says Leslie. "I couldn't explain what came over me. I guess it was love. He had trusted me with so much, and now he needed me to trust him. So I gave up fighting."

She told him everything—all the lies, all the dirt she had swept under the rug of her life, and finally why he couldn't get involved with that horrible man. Then she waited silently to see how he would react. John just stared at her and then tears came to his eyes. He held out his hand and took hers. He thanked her for trusting him with all her secrets and then he said, "I don't care about any of that. I trust you even more now for telling me. I have just one more question for you. Will you marry me?"

Leslie was flabbergasted. She spent so many nights imagining all the horrible things he could say to her if he ever knew about her past. But she never in her wildest dreams could have imagined this. "Still wanting to marry me after all that and without even needing to hear any explanation for why I did the things I did was like a dream," says Leslie. "Of course I said yes."

The power of faith came through for the two of them as John immediately severed ties with the rogue lawyer and worked to have him successfully disbarred. With John's loving support, Leslie had the courage to go to the authorities with all she knew about him, and he was convicted of murder and several other counts including extortion and fraud a decade later. John and Leslie finally tied the knot in 1989 in an incredibly romantic ceremony on top of the Strait of Gibraltar.

Then John sold his law practice, Leslie sold her last few houses, and they both gave it all up to move to Africa, where they became missionaries helping poor and hungry children see a better life.

"When the priest asked me to say 'I do' while we were standing up on that cliff in Gibraltar, somebody in the crowd yelled out, 'Don't jump!' " remembers Leslie. "I yelled back, 'I already did.' Trusting John was a real leap of faith for me, but I can't imagine what my life would be like today if I hadn't."

CHAPTER SIX

◆ The Principle of Devotion

" 'Mother' has always been a generic term synonymous with love, devotion, and sacrifice."

—Erma Bombeck

Turn on any one of those late-night talk shows some evening, and chances are you'll see beautiful celebrities talking all about how great life is now that they have all the money and fame they've ever wanted. Open up the newspaper, read your favorite magazine, or go to the movies, and you'll be bombarded with an avalanche of those same images of the rich and famous. In fact, just about everywhere you turn in modern-day society, you get the message that happiness is about becoming so successful that you can have whatever your heart desires. This egocentric, media-fueled mind-set doesn't leave much room for the principles of self-sacrifice and devotion that heroes know are essential.

After a while, this obsession with the self can really get to us. The "religion of egoism" starts to seep into our brain, and we begin to believe in it. We start to think that maybe life really *is* all about achieving the personal power that seems to make all these smiling, self-centered people so fulfilled. After all, it's hard to argue with that kind of in-your-face success. We soon forget that the whole point of our lives is to live for humanity in general, not just to focus on our own astronomical achievements so we can get our picture on the cover of *People* magazine or hang out with Oprah Winfrey.

Sure, celebrities accumulate impressive amounts of wealth and power, but what we don't see is who they had to hurt or desert to get where they are. Often, these "successful" people are filled with loneliness and emotional deprivation. As a former entertainment reporter, let me assure you it's not a pretty picture.

This erroneous belief system is what I refer to as the Hollywood Habit. It's an addiction to *me,* spread most successfully by the glossy images of Hollywood stars, parading their personal wealth and success on TV every night and especially at awards shows devoted to showcasing the rewards of self-devotion and self-gratification. And it is responsible for an escalating and disturbing culture of materialism and self-indulgence.

The Hollywood Habit promotes the belief that our purpose and greatest goal in life is to make money and serve our desires. The Hollywood Habit preaches self-gratification, self-worth, self-absorption, and self-determination. That is of course in direct opposition to the idea of heroism, which says our goal is to spread love, using money and work as a means to that end. Obviously, we should love ourselves, but not *only* ourselves.

This millionaire mind-set is all about human separatism and egoism. It twists the need to love and respect ourselves, so we can shine for others into an obsession with the self. Sacrifice is no longer for the sake of others; now it's only for one's own goals. This mind-set is deadly to individuals and to society on the whole. Can you imagine an entire society filled with self-seeking individualists only looking out for ways to get rich off of others? What if everybody bought into those get-rich-quick kits on TV that promise millions of dollars without us ever needing to really work again? Civilization would come to a screeching halt. These misguided souls espouse a philosophy that's in direct opposition to the concept of devoting oneself to others—one of the most important and crucial elements of heroism and happiness, and one of the founding principles of America.

What Is Devotion?

◈ *The heroic principle of devotion is the utter dedi-* cation and loyalty to another individual for the sake of helping that person through some great spiritual, physical, or even intellectual battle. It has nothing to do with what you get out of the relationship, although what you receive in the long run is extraordinary. Almost everyone has probably had the opportunity to experience the principle of devotion firsthand— whenever we take care of a sick child or a parent, when we take the time to guide a friend through turmoil in his or her life, or even when we stand by a spouse through a career or life transition.

Although egoists will argue that only focusing on our own ambition will bring about success, in the long run, the temporal rewards of ambition—namely money and power—can come and go all too easily. On the other hand, the reward of devotion is devotion of others to you, which is a bond that is so powerful it can overcome all of life's challenges even death itself and result in greater happiness than any celebrity or tycoon could ever buy.

Devotion is a long-term reciprocal bond with another, in which you commit your energy to helping them. In order to be loyal to another, the concept of self-sacrifice is necessary. That might mean giving your time, your energy, your resources, or something else of value to help another human being. Basically, it means that you are giving the best of yourself to help another. But that *doesn't* mean you cause your own self-destruction in the process. Although people who are devoted to another might sometimes risk their lives, it is with the hope (usually the educated hope) that they will survive. As is the case with all these tenets of heroism, self-abusive behavior is never part of the package. In order to truly devote yourself to another, you must maintain your strength and well-being so you can do the utmost to help that individual—it's only logical. The blind cannot lead the blind, and a drowning man cannot save another drowning man.

That said, devotion is not convenient. True devotion is given whenever the person needs it. It means you will be there for that person through thick and thin, in sickness and in health. Similarly, devotion does not drain or expect anything from the individual whom one is devoted to. In other words, you are not devoting yourself in order to get anything in return. Devotion is not a win–win dynamic, like so many modern sales gurus talk of. This is one of the most dangerous and misleading philosophies ever conceived of in personal morality, because it implies that you should only help someone when you know beyond the shadow of a doubt that it will help you to win, too. The only goal in devotion is the betterment of that individual. You might know down deep that the person you are helping is someone who will help you in the future when you need it, but that is not and cannot be the reason for your devotion. It must be unconditional love that is offered.

How Can I Bring Devotion into My Life?

So why should one even bother with such a difficult and selfless act? It is for the best of all reasons—out of genuine love for that individual. Of all the principles of heroism, devotion is the one that connects individuals most deeply in the bonds of human love. Therefore, to experience devotion, whether on the giving or the receiving end, allows one to experience the greatest grace and joy that love can deliver. In the end, it produces a greater result for both individuals than could ever have been realized alone. The deep and constructive life-giving bonds devotion develops are the backbone of marriage, family, and community. Devotional relationships were the basis of clans and countries, and they are still the basis for many treaties and alliances.

Without devotion we would help someone only when it would give us immediate gratification or payback. Because it's impossible for every single event between two people to equally benefit each individual every time, nobody would ever commit themselves to long-term support and coalition with another. All real and lasting relationships would be impossible.

So how do heroes do it? Well, devotion is more something that we need to be ready to do than something we can make part of our lives. Devotion is found in the relationships with the people we love, and every day we are probably overlooking opportunities with the people closest to us in our lives—our spouses, our children, our families, and our friends. And to experience it we simply must be ready to bear whatever burdens and hardships it requires to help a loved one. At times it can be an incredibly difficult cross to bear, but one that we must accept without reservation if we are sincerely devoted to someone. This is where we must fight to reject the principles and goals of all those TV tycoons we opened this chapter talking about. The more we begin to believe in social Darwinism and the theory that "only the strong survive," the less time we spend being devoted to each other. Looking only for how we will benefit, how we will prosper, and how we will make it to the top makes devotion impossible. Likewise, marriage becomes unworkable, family becomes unwieldy, and society disintegrates. Devotion is that important.

Unfortunately, much of the time our society promotes the belief that anything that detracts us from success is a liability and not healthy for us. We are taught to focus on ourselves by modern-day snake-oil salesmen selling us selfishness but deceptively calling it "success." They try to convince us that we need to be constantly focused on our own productivity.

But in actuality, thinking so much about ourselves and our success doesn't help us grow. On the contrary, it retards our growth because it isolates us, reducing the resources and relationships we have access to. Confronting and embracing people who need us most will bestow on us some of the greatest gifts life has to offer. Through the process of devotion, we learn to practice all the other principles in this book, as we connect ourselves to others with our ability to love—even when it isn't easy to do so, and even when there's nothing in it for us.

Although we don't expect anything back from those we heroically devote ourselves to, we usually get plenty of love in return and often find our devotions reciprocated when we need it most—and when we least expect it. That's when we find out who *our* heroes really are. That's exactly what a devoted mom discovered after she risked her life for her unborn son.

HOPEFULLY DEVOTED TO YOU

Robyn Bowen was twenty-two years old, and more than anything she and her new husband, Greg, wanted a baby. She was a hairstylist, he was an engineer at Motorola, and together they did well for such a young couple. The future looked bright, and they were enjoying their wedded bliss living in the sunny suburbs of Phoenix, Arizona, and looking forward to having a family. But no matter how hard they tried, and how much they prayed, it didn't seem to be in the stars for the young pair. "I shed many a tear because I was starting to believe that I was incapable of getting pregnant," remembers Robyn. "All the tests said it was possible, but no matter what we did, it wasn't happening."

A year later, the couple still wasn't pregnant, and doctors could find no medical reason for their failure. But during a routine check-up, doctors found something worse. Robyn was informed that she had a rare kidney disease for which there was no cure and no treatment. She would eventually die without a transplant. "Those words stuck in my heart like a cold, sharp sword," says Robyn. "I just sat there with tears streaming down my face. I didn't know what to think or feel and I just went numb."

"Glonerular sclerosis" was the technical name for this horrible disease. Robyn wasn't feeling any symptoms yet, but doctors said it was just a matter of time. The only good news was that she could still have a child. But her doctor warned her she had better hurry up and do it before complications from her disease set in and made pregnancy prohibitive.

"It was music to my ears to hear that I could still have a baby, and it made me want to have a child that much more, because now I knew the time to do it was running out," says Robyn. "But we were doing all we could, and without any success. I knew if we didn't make it happen soon, it wasn't going to happen," says Robyn.

The couple went on with their day-to-day lives as best as they could, working while doctors continued tests on Robyn. Although she still felt fine, she knew it was just a matter of time before the disease took its toll. Every day and every night she prayed that she would get pregnant. But as each month passed with no success, she thought a little less about it. Finally she decided to leave it in God's hands and go about her business dealing with her condition and the rest of her life.

Meanwhile, Robyn, who was a singer in the church choir, was getting ready to go on a musical tour with the group. It was around that same time her doctor suggested she make plans to travel to the renowned Mayo Clinic in Minnesota later that year for tests, because this facility had specialists who knew more about her condition. She was in the middle of making all her many travel plans for the coming months when something incredible happened—she discovered she was pregnant. "That day was the happiest day of my life," says Robyn. "God truly works in mysterious ways. We weren't even trying anymore, but everybody says that's how it works. I figured that meant God really wanted me to have a baby."

Robyn and Greg were on top of the world. In all the excitement and happiness, she almost forgot about her medical condition. But she was quickly reminded a few months later when it came time to go to the Mayo Clinic for her long-awaited appointment. "I was feeling so good about life after I found out I was pregnant," says Robyn, "and I figured maybe there was another miracle in store for me at the Mayo Clinic." Robyn held out hope that maybe the doctors in Minnesota knew something her doctors at home didn't. Maybe there was a cure. She could always hope and pray.

After several long and grueling days enduring test after test in the cold and sterile clinic, the doctors confirmed her condition, but they didn't have any comforting revelations for her. There was still no cure and still no treatment. Robyn would eventually need a transplant. But to make matters worse, tests showed that the disease was already beginning to affect her. They predicted that her kidneys would begin failing within months, not years. "The news wasn't good," says Robyn, "but it wasn't anything I wasn't prepared for."

But as she was sitting up on the exam table listening to her test results, the doctor said something much worse than she ever could have been prepared for. He bluntly told her to abort her child. "He said it almost casually," remembers Robyn. "He wasn't even really looking at me; he said it like it was just some matter-of-fact thing. I was in shock." The doctor informed Robyn that he believed continuing her pregnancy would most likely put so much stress on her failing kidneys that it would kill her, and that the only logical solution would be to have an abortion now, before it threatened her life.

Robyn sat completely still, staring at the doctor in disbelief. "It was like it didn't mean anything to him," remembers Robyn. "He didn't even try to say it gently or talk about options. He acted like killing my child was just a procedure." As tears welled up in her eyes, she pulled herself together enough to speak, but the words were hard to find. It took a few seconds, but then she summoned the strength to blurt them out. "That is absolutely not an option," she told him as bluntly as he had issued his proclamation moments before.

Robyn stormed out of the examination room, dressed herself quickly in the next room, and left the clinic immediately without saying another word. The next day she returned home to Phoenix, where she ran straight to her own doctor and demanded an explanation why he never warned her of the danger that now was unavoidable. "I wanted to know why he never told me that it was such a risk all that time while I was trying to get pregnant," says Robyn. "If I knew that before I got pregnant, of course I wouldn't have risked my baby's life or my own." The doctor did his best to comfort her, claiming the disease had progressed much more rapidly than he expected it would have. But that wasn't much help to Robyn now. She was faced with the decision of aborting her child almost four months into her pregnancy or risking her life to carry her child to term.

She knew it wouldn't be an easy road, but Robyn knew what she had to do. "If he had told me before I got pregnant, I could have prevented it," explains Robyn. "But he told me as long as I got pregnant soon it would be alright. Now it was too late.

There was a child inside of me who my husband and I prayed for. I wasn't going to turn my back on that baby, even if I had to risk my life. I told him then and there, 'I'm having this baby.' "

The pressure mounted as Robyn's pregnancy developed. The doctor kept constant watch over her condition, hoping that she would give birth before her kidneys began to fail. But there was no way of knowing exactly how long her kidneys would hold up. In the meantime, all they could do was hope and pray. "Not knowing was the most nerve-wracking part of it all," explains Robyn, "but I made the decision to stick by my child, and there was no turning back now. I just prayed God would help me through."

As scared as she was, nothing could put a damper on the love the young expectant mother was already feeling in her heart for her unborn baby, and every time he kicked, it reminded her. Robyn tried to keep her mind off the danger by doing all the things moms-to-be do—buying baby clothes, having a baby shower, and dreaming of how wonderful it would be to finally hold her baby in her arms.

Robyn was due to deliver on March 7, and when January rolled around with still no sign of trouble, she was beginning to feel more confident. But by the end of the month, her blood pressure was shooting sky-high and she was feeling tired all the time. She realized something was wrong, and it wasn't hard to guess what. "What else could it have been but my kidneys?" says Robin. "Still, I hoped I was wrong." But kidney function tests confirmed that her organs were beginning to fail, and it wouldn't be long before the strain the baby put on her body began to threaten her life. "That's when I really started to get scared," remembers Robyn. "I was prepared when I made the decision to stick by my baby that maybe I would die. But when you are face to face with that actually happening, it's terrifying. There's nothing you can really do about it except pray and hope that the doctors know what they are doing."

Robyn was immediately put on total bed rest, hoping she could ride it out until she delivered. But within a week, her kidneys were shutting down. Her ankles were the size of grapefruits, and Robyn was in constant pain. Finally, her doctor made the tough but unavoidable decision to deliver her child three weeks early. It was the only hope for the child and for Robyn. "He assured me it was the only choice I could make," says Robyn. "And he promised me that the child would be fine."

But the procedure wasn't easy. In Robyn's weak state, any extreme trauma could send her into a coma or shock, endangering her and her baby. Doctors began to induce labor at 9:30 A.M. on February 17, 1982. With every push Robyn grew weaker and weaker, as her body and her baby drained all the possible nutrients from her failing system. But Robyn was determined to hold on. For twelve hours, Robyn endured grueling labor, while doctors tried to feed her with nutrients to keep her alive. Then, just a few hours before midnight, Robyn delivered a beautiful and healthy five-pound, five-ounce baby boy named Brandon.

Robyn was exhausted. But when she saw her baby for the first time, she felt like she could have run a marathon for the chance to hold him close to her breast. "He was so beautiful, with such big blue eyes," recalls Robyn fondly. "I knew beyond the shadow of a doubt that I made the right decision. I could never have lived with myself if I had given up on him. That was the happiest day of my life." Amazingly, just a few days later, Robyn's kidneys started working again, allowing her to return home with her newborn bundle of joy and cherish all the pleasures of new motherhood.

The first years of Brandon's life were as blissful as could be. Robyn and her husband were consummate parents, reveling in his first smile, his first bath, baby teeth, teaching him to crawl, and his glorious first steps. Every mother cherishes those early memories of their first child, but for Robyn, they were just that much sweeter because she knew they might just as easily have never happened. "I probably doted on him because of that," says Robyn, "but I loved him with all my heart, and I was devoted to staying alive and staying well enough to raise him to be a happy and healthy adult."

But by the time Brandon was three years old, Robyn's kidneys stopped cooperating. Slowly but surely, Robyn grew sicker and sicker, until her kidneys were ready to give out. She was forced to start the painful dialysis treatments twice a week in order to stay alive, while doctors started to look for a kidney. "I was angry because I didn't want anything to take me away from my son," says Robyn. "Sure, nobody wants to die, but it wasn't the death that terrified me as much as leaving Brandon. I committed myself to his life and welfare before he was born, and I had to hang on."

As Robyn's condition worsened, her dialysis treatments were increased to three times a week for three hours a session. While her husband worked hard to keep up with the mounting medical bills, she took care of Brandon, never letting her illness get in the way and even taking him along with her as often as possible to dialysis instead of taking him to a sitter. Stuck full of needles and tubes, she'd entertain her son by reading to him and telling him stories while hiding the pain as much as possible.

But Robyn was growing weaker with every passing day. By 1985, doctors feared that if she didn't get a transplant soon, she'd be dead. "It wasn't looking good at that point," remembers Robyn. "They were telling me I had maybe a few months left if we didn't find something." Friends and family had already been tested to see if they might have the kidney to save Robyn's life, but to no avail. The organ banks couldn't deliver a match, either. But with time running out, doctors had no choice but to perform the transplant with the closest relative they could find. Robyn's mother, Mimi, volunteered to save her daughter's life. "When they told me she was giving me her kidney, I was stunned because I didn't even know hers would work," says Robyn. "But I couldn't have been more grateful. I had risked my life to save my child, and now here she was saving mine. It was pretty amazing."

The operation went off without a hitch, and Robyn felt like a million bucks again. She thought maybe now the worst was over. She could finally get back to raising the son she loved. For the next several years, Robyn devoted almost every waking hour to Brandon, hoping to make up for some of the time she lost while in and out of the hospital and thankful that now she could always be there for him. But by the time he was ready to enter school in 1987, Robyn was feeling sick again. Tests confirmed her worst fears—the kidney was being rejected. Within a few months, she was back on dialysis and fighting for her life.

Time was the enemy for Robyn now, as she struggled to hang on to life until she could find another donor. There were times when she felt like just giving in and giving up, but every time she looked at her son's smiling face it gave her courage and reason to hang on. Robyn tried to shield her son from the day-to-day struggles of her disease, even telling Brandon she didn't want him to come to her dialysis treatments anymore. Now that he was old enough to understand what was happening, she thought it would be too depressing. But he insisted that he wanted to be there. "He helped me endure a lot," says Robyn. "I might not have made it if I didn't know that there was this beautiful little boy there who needed me to get well."

With still no exact match in sight for Robyn, in 1989 another emergency transplant with a close match from an anonymous donor was a temporary reprieve. The transplant bought Robyn a year of relief, but soon that kidney also failed, and it was back to dialysis.

Meanwhile, things weren't going well for Robyn and Greg's marriage. Whether it was the stress of Robyn's illness or that the two grew apart over the years, something wasn't working. The couple got a divorce in 1993. Now it was just Robyn and Brandon.

A single mom, Robyn made the best home she could for her son. She found a job she could do from home—processing medical bills—which gave her as much time as possible to spend with her son. Robyn worked during the mornings, then picked up Brandon from school and off they both went to her dialysis, then back home.

A few years later, Robyn fell in love with Stephen, one of her dialysis technicians, and they got married in 1996. Being married to her dialysis technician, she could now receive her treatments at home, allowing her and Brandon to sit together after school in the privacy of their own home while she received her treatments, talking and sharing, and just getting to know each other.

As Brandon got older and as Robyn grew sicker, he became more and more concerned about his mother. Then one day he asked her a question she never thought she would hear. He wanted to know if one of his kidneys might just be the answer to end her agony. The question floored Robin. "The last thing in the world I wanted was for him to give me a kidney," says Robyn. "I didn't even really respond to him. I figured he would just forget about it."

Robyn grew weaker and weaker waiting for a kidney that would be a match. And the chance of her getting one became less and less likely, as her body developed more antibodies due to the slow rejection of the kidney inside her. As the years went by, Robyn hung on, bolstered by the love of her new husband and, of course, Brandon's ceaseless love and support. But there was no way to stop the disease from continuing to ravage her body.

When Brandon was fourteen years old, he finally asked his mother if he could get tested to see if he could save her life. "I thought he had forgotten all about it," says Robyn. "So I told him he wasn't old enough. I figured that would put an end to it." But every few months he would ask again if he could get tested as he watched his mother suffer. Every time, Robin would put him off, hoping he would stop asking.

Watching her son grow up into a fine young man gave Robyn strength. Brandon was active in his church, a good student, and hardworking. As Brandon entered his senior year in high school, Robyn's health seriously deteriorated. She knew if she didn't find another kidney soon, she might not live to see her son graduate. "I had pretty much come to the end," reveals Robyn. "I had lost almost fifty pounds, and I was so weak I really didn't even want to eat anything. But I promised Brandon I would see him graduate. At some point, wanting to keep that promise was the only thing that kept me going."

Robyn kept her promise. Right after graduation, Brandon gave his mom a hug and told her he had a surprise. He was going to get tested to see if he could save her life. "I didn't know what to say," remembers Robyn. "I didn't want him to do it, but he insisted. He said he loved me, and that this is what you're supposed to do when you love someone."

Brandon felt sure that he would be a match, but when the test results came back, he was only a half-match, with a positive "cross-match"—a technical term referring to certain antibody reactions that made a transplant impossible. "Brandon was devastated when he got the news," says Robyn. "But I was kind of relieved. It was heartbreaking to think my son was going to have to risk surgery to save my life. At least this way it wasn't even an issue. But I couldn't help but be overcome by his desire to give me that kind of a gift."

Robyn fought on, but the situation was bleak. After two unsuccessful transplants, it was almost impossible to secure a donor for a third. There were more than 500 people in Arizona alone waiting for a kidney transplant, and the decision to grant someone a kidney was based on a combination of factors, the most important of which was the chances of survival and the likelihood of rejection. In Robyn's condition and with her record, she wasn't high on the list. Robyn was prepared for the worst. "I was so happy that I'd kept my promise to see Brandon graduate," says Robyn. "I certainly didn't want to die, but at least I knew now that he was old enough to take care of himself and that he would be okay if I did."

But Brandon wasn't about to give up on his mom. When he heard of an experimental transplant procedure using half-matches with positive cross-matches, he was ready to try it to save his mom. But the procedure was dangerous, and it had only been performed a handful of times so far. Robyn was flattered that her son was willing to risk so much to save her, but she couldn't stand the thought of him putting his life on the line. "There was no way I was going through with it unless those doctors assured me that nothing would happen to him," remembers Robyn. "My own doctor didn't recommend it. He thought it was too dangerous."

But Brandon knew it was his mother's only real chance, and he was ready to take the risk. As Robyn grew sicker and sicker, Brandon pressured his mother to accept his offer. Finally, she agreed.

A month later, mother and son checked into the Mayo Clinic in Rochester, Minnesota—the same clinic Robyn had stormed out of eighteen years earlier, pregnant with the son they told her she should never have. "We were going back to that same place where I decided to save his life, only now it was the other way around," remembers Robyn.

As mother and son lay on gurneys next to each other before being wheeled off into separate operating rooms, Robyn made one last attempt to talk her son out of it. "I told him he could quit right then and there and nobody would mind, especially not me," explains Robyn. "I really still couldn't bring myself to totally accept this." But Brandon just smiled and told his mom he was going through with it no matter what.

After they wheeled her son out, she asked to see the doctor. When he arrived, Robyn had a stern warning for him. "I pulled him down by the collar and looked him straight in the eye and I said, 'You promise me right here and now that you will personally make sure he comes out of this okay.'" The doctor agreed, and moments later, mother and son both went under the knife.

The next morning, Robyn woke up to a bright and beautiful May morning. She immediately asked about her son. He was fine. They both were. The operation was a rousing success. Brandon had saved Robyn's life.

"I never in a million years would have wished that upon him," says Robyn. "I still can't believe he did that for me. He's the greatest son any mom could ever ask for."

But to Brandon it was a no-brainer. Says Brandon, "I always knew that someday I would need to save my mother's life. After all, she's my mom, and I wouldn't even be here today if it wasn't for her risking *her* life for *me*."

A year later, Robyn and Brandon are both doing great, and Robyn has shown no signs of rejection. And both mother and son continue to be *hopefully* devoted to each other.

CHAPTER SEVEN

◆ The Principle of Altruism

"The beginnings of altruism can be seen in children as early as the age of two. How then can we be so concerned that they count by the age of 3, read by 4, and walk with their hands across the overhead parallel bars by 5, and not be concerned that they act with kindness to others?"

—Neil Kurshan, *Raising Your Child to Be a Mensch*

*Remember how you gave up buying that brand-*new car so you could afford to send your daughter to those ballet lessons she had been begging for? Or the time you sacrificed tickets to the big game so you could go see your son play in his big game? Or the day you politely gave up your standby seat on an airplane and took a later flight, just so the elderly woman behind you could fly—even though the airline wasn't offering any incentive to do so? And then there are all those times you complimented people throughout the day. Or the simple way you always hold the door for the person coming behind you. Or those donuts you bring into the office for everybody to share. Or the way you always give your brother a Christmas gift, even though he never remembers to give you one.

Hats off to you, for in the simplest and easiest of everyday ways, you are promoting altruism—the belief that our motives should be to help others in everything we do. And you don't do it because you want anything in return, you don't do it for recognition, and you don't even do it because you think the recipient has earned it. You do it simply to comfort and help out another human being. Remember how wonderful you felt when you saw the giant smile come across the face of the person you helped? Not that you expected anything in return, not even a smile, but it sure was nice to get one.

If that wasn't you in the above scenarios, wake up and smell the kindness. This world we live in depends on it. If you agree with the starting premise of this book, that we were created to love and that caring about others is the only way to find happiness, then you have no logical choice but to be an altruist.

※ SEE TRUEBLOOD
RE: THE MEANING
of LIFE

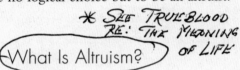

What Is Altruism?

Altruism and compassion are similar, but they have one very meaningful difference. Unlike with compassion, the people an altruist helps don't necessarily have to be experiencing any kind of pain or noticeable misfortune—although they may be. But the point of altruism is not simple benevolence or charity. It is an obligation to sacrifice one's own interests for the sake of the good of others. You are not responding to human suffering to make you act; you are simply reaching out and touching another human being with kindness and human favor, just because it's the right thing to do. This is what makes altruism probably one of the noblest of the virtues of heroes, because the heroic altruist doesn't really have any necessary and noticeable cue that somebody needs help. The altruist is simply responding to the reality that, in general, people need people. We all have to touch each other in order for this giant phenomenon known as humanity to work the way it's supposed to.

The heroic altruist understands that, like all these other principles, altruism is an important part of the cycle of life. And ironically, only by giving freely of ourselves and expecting nothing in return can we *all* reap happiness and success in the long run. In the end, there is no reason to not be altruistic.

How Can I Bring Altruism into My Life?

In order to understand how to make altruism a part of our daily lives, it's first important to understand why everybody doesn't necessarily practice altruism already. Why wouldn't they, if it is indeed such a logical way to live? Once we realize how and why we sometimes forget to be altruists then we see a little more clearly all the ways we can make altruism part of our everyday lives.

First of all, maybe we just don't think about it. It's rather easy to get so wrapped up in our own problems and concerns that we don't notice others right in front of us who we could inspire and fulfill so easily with just a little bit of consideration and effort. Courtesy, one of the simplest forms of altruism, is one of the victims of this modern mindlessness we find ourselves in today. Take, for example, the simple act of saying "please" and "thank you." There's certainly nothing very difficult about it, and most people agree it's appropriate and worthwhile, yet how many times do we forget to do it? That's easy enough to fix. Just slow down and take the time to notice there's a human being right next to you most of the time. Simply be polite.

Second, maybe we are afraid to help others. The media have filled our heads with so many stories of murder and mayhem that many of us are afraid to step out the door each day, let alone stop and interact with someone we hardly know. Or maybe we have a very real and sensible concern for our safety, say in a big city where it's impossible to know all of your neighbors and feel safe interacting with strangers on the street. That's certainly reasonable enough, except it raises the greater question of why we create social situations in which we are so isolated from our neighbors that we need to be weary of them. This whole phenomenon is a little more difficult to deal with, but it isn't beyond repair. Altruism is attainable, even within this mind-set. Just apply the remedy for the last objection a little bit further. We *must* slow down and notice the people around us, then get to know them. We need to take the time to see our friends, family, neighbors, colleagues, and even people on the streets as human beings who possess all the same emotions, concerns, fears, and loves that we do. Once we accomplish that, we can communicate and bond with them through those commonalties. Eventually, the barriers of fear, hatred, and hurtfulness will dissipate and be replaced with our common goal of happiness. Again I stress we *must make* the time to do this every day in our hustle and bustle lives, not just occasionally when it is convenient for us to do so.

The third obstacle to altruism is much more emblematic of a social phenomenon that runs deep in our society—the assembly line syndrome. Stopping to help someone else on that line can be disastrous to your well-being and personal success, plus it could bring down the whole system. We've made our society so competitive that we are afraid to give up our edge, even with friends, family, and work colleagues.

So anything that would help the next guy over us is out of the question, right? Wrong. This is actually the easiest of the arguments against altruism to dismiss, because the hero knows this product-oriented way of looking at life and the world around us is not logical because it is not consistent with the way we were designed to be. Refuting it is a matter of dismissing the belief as invalid, and realizing that acting altruistically will not threaten your livelihood but quite the contrary Once again, if we are designed to love each other and doing so brings us joy and happiness, then helping others will increase our joy even if it doesn't increase our productivity or finances. But even those temporal concerns will fare better in the long run with altruism because the general morale of society will be higher.

All these obstacles to altruism motivate us to distance ourselves from others. The heroes among us have rejected these objections, either because of their upbringing or because they have seen firsthand that serving others is not hazardous to your health.

Nevertheless, these altruistic heroes are not foolhardy people who don't care at all about their own success or safety. They never senselessly subject themselves or their families and friends to a dangerous situation. They simply practice a sensible degree of precaution. Then, after an intelligent assessment of any risks, they spring into action reaching out to others. They know there are intelligent, rational, and safe ways to help.

Similarly, heroes are not penniless paupers who give away all they have until they can no longer take care of themselves. Altruists work hard and creatively to provide well for themselves, their families, and their communities so they can give even more of their support and resources to others.

Altruism is one of the noblest forms of heroism. But in practicing altruism, there can be a danger of becoming so wrapped up in doing for others that you stop taking care of your own responsibilities. The safeguards for that are twofold. First, look at why you are helping. Is it part of a healthy plan of living a full and balanced heroic life serving *all* the principles of heroism? Or is it a co-dependant addiction to helping others for some dangerous and selfish self-validation or to avoid carrying your own load in life? Only you can tell yourself if your motives are pure. After all, the point of being a hero is not simply to live for others, but to live for humanity, which of course includes your own, too. Besides, only after we have taken care of our simple needs can we truly help anyone else.

There are countless examples of altruistic heroes in our midst. Like Oral Lee Brown, an Oakland Realtor who made a modest living and was preparing to retire when she decided to walk into Brookfield Elementary School twelve years ago and promised a class of first-grade students she would pay for them all to go to college. Twelve years later, at fifty-two years old, she made good on that promise, beginning to pay the tuition of those now-grown children as they entered their freshman year in colleges from coast to coast.

Or like Matel Dawson, who toiled as a forklift driver for Ford Motor Company in Dearborn, Michigan, for almost sixty years. All that time he saved his pennies, and after he retired, he donated more than a million dollars of his savings to universities all across the Unites States for scholarships.

Or the simple example of the Firehouse Flower Lady, who for months spent several hours a night taking care of all the bouquets and notes left in homage to the New York City Fire Department after the September 11, 2001, attacks.

Then there is the amazing story of Secret Santa. His extraordinary acts of kindness and unsolicited giving, for no other reason than to spread the spirit of altruism wherever he goes, make the world a brighter place, one heart at a time.

SAMARITAN SANTA

In the winter of 1971, somewhere down in the land of Mississippi, there lived a young and hardworking salesman who we'll call John, because nobody knows his real name. John was a charming man who had a way with people. And he knew how to sell.

People trusted the door-to-door salesman when he came their way with his wares. And he trusted people, too, like his boss, who kept a watchful eye on John's efforts from the home office a couple states away. Every day John sold his heart out, and he trusted that in return each week his boss would send him his check and pay the rent on the tiny hotel room he used as an office.

But then one day the checks stopped coming, the rent didn't get paid, and the motel kicked John out. Unbeknownst to the young go-getter, his employer had gone out of business without thinking to inform John. Just like that, the young and hard-working salesman was out in the cold. "I can tell you from experience that people don't usually wind up homeless because they want to be," says John. "One minute I was working and paying my bills, and the next thing I knew I was on the street."

Confused and scared, young John slept in his car, naively waiting and hoping for the delinquent payments from his boss to arrive. "I kept believing that there must have been a mix-up or something at first," says John. By the time he finally realized the money wasn't coming, he was broke with nowhere to turn for help. "After about a week, I realized what was happening. But by then I used up all my money."

John turned to the only place in the small town he felt might assist him, the local church. But when he was turned away because the social services director was already gone for the day, John couldn't help but feel like the world had tossed him out for good. "It's hard enough to swallow all your pride and get up the guts to admit to a stranger that you're broke and need help," says John, "but you really feel like a failure when you get turned down on top of that. Then you've hit rock bottom."

After two days without food and another cold night sleeping in the car that he couldn't even buy gas for, the young man was just about all out of hope and all out of options. Desperate and hungry, John was ready to do just about anything for a buck or a hot meal. The next morning he cleaned himself up in a public bathroom, then he walked into the local diner and sat down to eat without so much as a dime in his pocket. "I was starving to death, and I didn't care one bit at that point if I could pay for it or not," admits John. "I simply had no place else to go."

Realizing that it might be quite a while before his next meal, John ordered a feast and ate until he could eat no more. When the bill came due, he put his plan to dine-and-dash into action, pretending he'd lost his wallet and all his cash. "I put on an Academy Award–winning performance," recalls John. "I turned that restaurant upside down looking everywhere, even outside, too, like I really was determined to find it." When John was sure he had pulled off his caper, he got ready to make his escape.

But that's when a miracle happened, as John sees it, one that would change his life and the lives of so many others forever. As John got ready to make a clean break for it, the owner, who was also the restaurant's cook, emerged from behind the counter and walked behind John. Then he reached down to the ground and seemed to pick something up off the floor. He stood back up, looked John square in the eye, smiled, and said, "Son, you must have dropped this on the way in," as he handed John a crisp, new $20 bill. John was stunned beyond any response.

"That was a fortune to me," remembers John. "I couldn't believe I got this lucky—to have this guy find $20 on the floor that someone else obviously dropped and for him to think it was mine. I figured I better get out of there fast before someone came back looking for the cash they lost."

John frantically snatched up the money and paid the bill, then he darted out the front door. He pushed his car to a gas station so he could fill up and get out of town fast before anyone got wise to him. With a full tank and a full stomach, plus a few dollars extra in his pocket, he headed west for Kansas City, hoping to land a job and make a fresh start in the big city. Meanwhile, he kept wondering about whether the person who actually dropped the money had ever returned for it.

That's when it hit John that maybe nobody had dropped any money at all. Could it actually have been the owner who took the money out of his own pocket and pretended John dropped it so he could help him out? "You didn't see too many $20 bills in those days just lying around on the floor," says John. "I figured that fella was just trying to help me out in a way that wouldn't embarrass me. Lord knows I'd been prayin' every day for a miracle, and it seemed like God really had been listening."

As John drove on into the night and gazed out at the open

road that lay ahead of him, he thought of the better life that lie ahead, too. He knew he'd been given a great gift, and as the tears welled up in his eyes, he made a promise to himself and to God. "I decided right then and there to pay back that favor," explains John. "I said 'Lord, if you ever put me in a position to do a good deed for other people the way that man helped me, then that's what I am going to do.' "

In Kansas City, John quickly landed another sales job and worked hard to get back on his feet. But it wasn't easy. Times were tough in the early 1970s, and like so many people, he lived paycheck to paycheck, struggling to make ends meet. But at least now he had a roof over his head and three square meals a day, all because of that helpful stranger.

A few years later, the ambitious salesman borrowed money to start a business and although he worked his fingers to the bone to make it successful, it failed. He struggled to pay back the loan. But John refused to give up his dreams, and a second idea for a company was a success. "I certainly didn't do it by myself," John insists, "I had help from a lot of supportive people along the way. No individual becomes a success all by himself."

As time passed, John did a little bit better for himself each year. He met a wonderful woman and they married. A few years later, the happy couple started a family. Things were good for John, and the pains of his past poverty faded away with his success. But the memory of the miracle that changed his life would never be forgotten. "If that man hadn't been so kind, I don't know what would have happened to me," admits John. "I might have done something really desperate and wound up in jail or worse. That man probably saved my life."

So in 1979, John decided it was time to step up to the promissory plate and follow through on the vow he made on that dark winter's night eight years before. It was time to start giving a little back. So a few days before Christmas, on a frigid night much like the one on which he made the promise, John pulled up to a little drive-in restaurant in Independence, Kansas, for a quick bite to eat. As he waited for his order, he noticed the young carhop who braved the icy elements to bring his order to his window looked so sad. In a way, she reminded John of himself so many years ago, so cold and alone, trying hard to make a living and make ends meet. He knew right then and there that this was where he could start his campaign for caring.

When it came time to pay the little over two-dollar bill, he gave the girl $50 and told her to keep the change. "You have no idea what this means to me," the young girl exclaimed between sobs as she held the change in her hand and looked into John's eyes. She thanked him over and over again, still hardly believing what had happened. "You should have seen her face light up when I told her it was no joke," recalls John. "It was as if that simple kind act changed her life in some way." It was only $50, but John felt like a million bucks. He headed right over to the bank and withdrew some more money so he could go give it away somewhere else.

John couldn't afford to give out too much that Christmas, but

he gave what he could throughout the holiday season to everyone from hardworking folks on the job to people on the street.
And every time he handed out an unexpected $20 or $50 to an
unsuspecting victim of his kindness, faces beamed with joy and
gratitude. Smiles spread from ear to ear and endless "Thanks!"
echoed in the wind as he drove off. "Who knows, maybe one of
those people was in the same shape I was in," says John. But it
really didn't matter what their situation was as long as they knew
someone cared. "All that's really important to me is that they
know they're not alone," says John, "and that they know people
are really good at heart."

For the next few years, every time Christmas rolled around
John got back into the giving spirit, handing out his casual cash
to strangers all over Kansas, wherever he might be at the time
he felt the desire. And amazingly, he never told anybody about
it either, not even his wife or family. "It was very important to
me that it be something I was not recognized for," says John. "I
was doing it because I wanted to be nice, and I hoped that concept could catch on with others, too. But if people knew it was
me, it could put the focus on who I was instead of what I was
doing. I didn't want anything to take emphasis away from the
gift of giving."

But within a few years his little secret—his little Secret Santa,
that is—was beginning to attract attention around town. Reporters were sent scurrying to uncover "Santa's" true identity.
That's when John decided to let his wife and family in on it.
They helped him keep his secret and turn it into something

grander than even he could have imagined. He devised a disguise loosely resembling a Santa outfit and headed out in a rented red van to do his altruistic good deeds.

As public awareness of the acts of Secret Santa grew in Kansas City each year, so did the size of John's generosity. He now was handing out $100 bills. Soon, he was collectively giving away thousands of dollars every year all over the state of Kansas, $100 at a time, to people like the man in the thrift store who was looking for a winter coat to brave the cold with only 75 cents to his name. Or the couple he heard haggling with the electric company on the pay phone in order to make a deal to turn their power back on. Santa gave them light for Christmas. Or the people doing their laundry on Christmas Eve, who all got a hundred bucks to stick in their freshly clean stockings. And then there was the restaurant where manna truly fell from the sky when Santa showed up with $100 for every customer and employee. And there were many more.

As the years passed and his ability to give increased, Santa got a little more sophisticated about his giving. He started working with local agencies to identify people with special needs who he could help. That's when the stories became nothing short of miraculous. There was $3,000 for the struggling family of the fourteen-year-old boy suffering from leukemia. A widow struggling to raise seven adopted children and two grandchildren opened her door and thought she was seeing things when Santa handed her twenty $100 bills. "Have a merry Christmas everybody," said Santa as he made his getaway from the crowded house to the satisfying sound of cheers coming from within. When Santa heard of a man on welfare who gave his own watch away as a Christmas present to his social worker, Santa gave the man a new watch and $2,000. And a young man who needed a lung transplant breathed a sigh of relief when Santa gave him $20,000—just like that.

Santa paid for rent, car payments, families' grocery bills, and legal bills—all without warning and without hanging around for praise. "My Christmas present is the look on their faces when I give them the money," says John. "It's probably against the law to feel this good, but I do it anyway."

By 1999, John was giving away more than $80,000 a year and loving every minute of it, leaving people behind blessing him and blessing God for his goodness.

But it's not just needy people who receive Santa's money. After all, much of the time Santa doesn't even know anything about the people he's helping. "I always hope that it's going to go to a good use," says John. "But most of the time I really have no control over that, and that's not the point of the gift. What they do with it is their business. I only ask that they pass on the giving spirit to someone else down the road if they can."

After a couple years playing Santa Claus, John was getting quite good at it. But there was one stocking he really wanted to fill—that of the man who was so kind to him so many years ago. So that year John set out to search for the $20 hero who saved his life. For almost a year he searched until he found the man. The diner had long since closed, but he was finally able to track down its former owner. John had found his Good Samaritan, and his name was Ted.

The eighty-one-year-old retired diner owner received a mysterious phone call one day from a man claiming to be a historical researcher, and he wanted longtime resident Ted's help. John arranged a meeting, and of course he came bearing gifts. "I'm that guy who you helped twenty-eight years ago," John revealed as he sat in Ted's living room and delivered his whopping surprise. "You never know what one little act of kindness can do for somebody," John told Ted. "It can change somebody's whole life. It changed mine when I got on the road and figured out what you did." Then Santa handed the man $10,000, leaving him speechless and shedding a few unavoidable tears of joy.

John had no way of knowing this, but the last few years had not been so kind to Ted. Ted's wife was very ill—within the last few years she had battled cancer, seriously broken her hip and leg, and now she was struggling with the horrible effects of Alzheimer's. The medical bills were piling up, and the insurance just wasn't enough. The money was a Godsend. "It was extraordinary," said John. "Here I was just trying to pay him back for his kindness, unaware of his situation just as he was unaware of mine back then. But it goes to show that you just never know where somebody is in their life. That's why it's so important to be kind all the time, and you never know when you will be a lifesaver."

Santa had repaid that debt, but his desire to give just kept on going. After the horrible terrorist attacks crippled New York

City on September 11, 2001, Santa decided to make a special Christmas visit to the Big Apple on the week before Christmas. While people all over the city pulled together to help each other, Santa hit the streets ready to dole out $25,000. There was the man just released from a hospital who didn't have any money to go back home to his family in Alabama. Santa handed him $300 for a ticket. There was the teenage security guard with a brand-new baby at home who got $100. And again there were the homeless, the hapless, the aged, and the sickly who got a helping hand. Plus a whopping $5,000 gift left at St. Paul's Chapel right across the street from Ground Zero, the church Mayor Giuliani called the Miracle Chapel because it didn't suffer a scrape when the World Trade Center collapsed. St. Paul's had been serving about 2,000 meals a day to relief workers, and the money was a huge help. Another $5,000 went to a social services agency, and thousands more was distributed all over the town.

Back in Kansas City, once again there were all the usual recipients unexpectedly presented with Santa's Christmas presents, as there will continue to be every year. And nowadays, John likes giving away money so much he's started to do it all year 'round, whenever he gets the urge in his heart to help. "There's a saying that I always remember," says John. "It goes, 'Blessed are those who forget not from where they came nor those they knew along the way.' I will never forget that. We all come from the same place, so we better remember each other all the time."

Now because word has gotten around the country and even

the world of Santa's good deeds, John says he receives e-mails all the time telling him how others have begun to follow his lead trying to devote their days and lives to giving to others. And that's all that Santa wants for his Christmas present—for people to remember to give to others. "There is no such thing as a self-made man," John says again. "People don't become successful all by themselves. You might think you are doin' it alone, but whether you realize it or not, if you make it, it's because there was somebody who was kind enough to give you a helping hand along the way. It's only right that we all keep reaching out our hands to others."

CHAPTER EIGHT

◆ The Principle of Compassion

Unbounded courage and compassion join'd,
Tempering each other in the victor's mind,
Alternately proclaim him good and great,
And make the hero and the man complete.

—Joseph Addison, *The Campaign*

◈ *Did you know that almost a quarter of the children* in this country go to bed hungry every night? That's a startling statistic, but it's true. Doesn't hearing that make you want to do something to help? That's what compassion is all about.

Have you ever been terminally ill? Or have you ever been so confused or depressed that you thought about ending your life? Ever been so poor you didn't know where your next meal was coming from or where you were going to sleep that night? If not, have you ever known anybody who was suffering like that?

Chances are, you answered "yes" to at least one of those questions. Because if you open your eyes, ears, and heart, you will probably encounter somebody down on his or her luck just about every day. Maybe it's a close friend you don't even

139

realize needs your help because you aren't paying attention. Or maybe it's a family member you've had a falling out with who is hurting, but you don't even notice their pain. It could be a stranger on the street you see with a sad story in their heart, or a child going to bed every night with tears of hunger in his eyes.

When you see an elderly woman struggling to open a door, most people will feel concern. But some will actually be so moved that they take a moment out of their day to help her through. When the homeless man on the street asks you for a dollar, will you look the other way, or will you genuinely try to help giving him advice or directions to a shelter where he can get a hot meal and some help? Regardless of the cause of his social, psychological, and physical ills, a hero shows a genuine desire and commitment to help relieve the pain of his fellow human beings.

What Is Compassion?

When most people hear of the plight of others less fortunate, we have a natural tendency to care. But sometimes that will make us want to do something to relieve their pain. This is compassion, and it's a natural outgrowth of our design to love. Even if you have been fortunate enough to never know hardships, you probably feel a pang in your heart when you hear of human misery, and you desire to help heal the hurt.

The heroic principle of compassion is a combination of this naturally occurring feeling of caring about somebody's pain, plus having the motivation of spirit to actually do something about relieving that person's discomfort.

But standing in the way of compassion is the prevalent tendency in modern society to turn away and distance ourselves from others' problems. This rejection of our natural desire to help is fueled by the same fears discussed in Chapter Seven about altruism—people wrongly assume that reaching out to someone else will somehow compromise their own safety or livelihood. This apathy for others is the source of great misery and madness in our world, because it flies in the face of our natural design and promotes the dehumanization of our society and our people.

Compassion plays a vital role in the world. Without the force of compassion, only the strong would survive. Those who fell by the wayside, even just for a short time, would simply be swept away under the weight of their own misfortune. If this were the case, none of the stories in this book, tales about people overcoming life's greatest hardships through the power of love, would have been possible. Think about yourself. Have you ever needed anyone because you were hurting physically, emotionally, mentally, spiritually, or financially? I guarantee there isn't one person reading this book who hasn't, at some point in their lives, needed someone to help them through some pain or struggle. If not for the concept and presence of compassion working in the world, each one of us would always have to fend for ourselves, even when times got tough. Everyone needs somebody sometimes to feel for them.

Our built-in program to help others in their time of need is an absolute component of our civilization. And the most important product of this compassion is not necessarily that we solve the person's problems, although we certainly try to help. The real result is that the recipient is convinced, by our supportive actions, that he or she is worthwhile—worthy of love. In this way, their value as a human being is reestablished. That is the true grace of compassion.

The bottom line: It is illogical for us to go through our lives so wrapped up in ourselves that we don't help others. From a purely pragmatic point of view, it's impossible that any one person exists who will never need another's help or comfort. Therefore, to not help others is to promote a way of life that will doom you when you need help. And it's unreasonable to act in any way that will potentially cause you harm somewhere down the line. Without compassion, there's no more society. With compassion in abundance, we create a loving utopia filled with joy and love. Obviously, our current society sits somewhere in between those two extremes.

Betty Sue Vista
Howard & Anil

How Can I Bring Compassion into My Life?

◈ So because compassion is such an important principle, how do we become more compassionate? One way is to reflect upon our own moments of need in the past. This will help us identify with others who are in need in the future. The route to understanding other human pain goes directly through your own. There are only so many human experiences, and at some point, there are so many common ones.

But the simple directive from which all compassion comes is to simply be sensitive and attentive. When you see someone suffering, don't fight your natural compulsion to help them. They are human beings worthy of all the dignity, respect, and compassion that requires.

This next aspect of practicing compassion is probably the hardest part, but the one that will truly make you a hero to someone who is down and out. Once you set out to show compassion, it is most important to view that person as a human being with innate value—not to be judged but simply appreciated, not to be fixed but simply comforted. In other words, a person deserves your compassion or help simply because they are a human being and they are hurting even if they have caused their misfortune themselves. Your goal is to show you care and to try and relieve the pain and suffering, but *not* to try to "fix" the person. This is the only way to truly exhibit compassion, and

* Very important: To help is not to fix.

143

it's the only way to reach the ultimate goal—convincing the recipient he or she is a worthwhile human being. Once they are convinced of this, they will be able to fix themselves. You can help show them the direction to go, but they ultimately will need to take the steps once they know that someone cares.

This point is especially important in the case of terminally ill patients. Once all the medical possibilities have been exhausted, we still must love and care for our loved ones just as stridently . . . even though it may never result in them getting any better. Our compassion focuses on simply loving someone who is hurting, not just trying to make them recover. That being said, miracles do frequently happen when people show such love.

Appreciating this brings us very conveniently right back to the premise of this book. Our purpose is to love each other, not for any other reason than that we are all human beings and worthy of love. Therefore, our purpose is to have compassion for every single human being we meet. Compassion is not earned, but everyone deserves it. It is our right and our responsibility.

In the end, heroes understand that loving humanity means caring about all human beings, no matter what their predicament, abilities, or insufficiencies are. That's something each of us can do every day of our lives if we stop focusing on what we want the world to look like and to be and concentrate instead on simply accepting and loving others as they are. Then we can allow people to be the best and brightest they can be because we have helped validate their worth by our respect and compassion. Once you remove all judgment and expectation and simply comfort your fellow man, the world of unconditional love will open up to you in ways you never imagined.

HOLY HELPER

When Sister Mary Kathleen Sheehan was just a little girl, one of nine children of Irish immigrant parents and growing up in the Boston suburbs, she already knew what she wanted to do with her life. Every Sunday when she saw the collection plate pass at church, she'd tell her mother that one day she was going to help those people. "God put us here on earth to have compassion for others," says Sister Mary. "We each have a different path to take in order to do that. Mine just happens to be to aid the poor, and I knew that was what I was supposed to do."

You probably have never heard of Sister Mary Kathleen Sheehan unless you are from Louisville, Kentucky, where she acts as the guardian angel to thousands of weary souls. A five-foot-one gray-haired *tour de force,* she is a soldier in the war on homelessness who changes lives every day, simply by having a heart and putting it to use. She is the executive director at the St. John's Day Center for Homeless Men, and she maintains that "our role here is to comfort and help the people who others don't even want to acknowledge, let alone care for. I'm sad to say that our nation treats people like products, and when they don't work we throw them out. Here at the center we must care for those throwaways and try to make them feel valuable again."

Sister Mary became a nun with the Sisters of Charity of

** of THE
ATTY. IN "DARWINIAN"
WHO FEELS THIS WAY.*

Nazareth when she was just twenty years old. The order relocated her to Louisville, where she first taught in one of the local Catholic grade schools. But Sister Mary knew she wasn't destined to teach; she wanted to help the poor, just like she promised when she was a little girl. It was the early 1970s, and the pope was calling for more clergy to get involved in social justice issues with Vatican II. So Sister Mary happily answered the call by going to work at a Catholic crisis center, assisting people who couldn't pay their rent or utilities. "So many of these people felt powerless," says Sister Mary. "They needed to know that someone cared about what was happening to them."

Many of the city's poor were living in deplorable conditions—in burned-out slums run by greedy and abusive landlords who took their tenants' money but forced them to live in unlivable buildings. Many of those slumlords let their buildings fall into such a state of disrepair that eventually everyone moved out. But scores of these burned-out and deserted buildings still stood, and the vacant structures soon became homes to drugs, murders, and mayhem. Meanwhile, the city refused to condemn them, largely because of the influence of their slumlord owners. Sister Mary was so moved by the plight of these neighborhoods and their desperate residents that she decided to tear down the vacant buildings herself—that is, with a little help from a few of her fellow sisters and priests, plus an uprising of concerned local citizens. Together, they stormed the abandoned buildings and starting dismantling them with their bare hands. "My superiors weren't too thrilled with that one," remembers Sister Mary, "but when I saw what was happening I had to do something about it."

Her protest helped bring about new laws and city programs to clear out the abandoned buildings and help revitalize the inner city. But it wasn't easy; Sister Mary was arrested for her protests against the slumlords. But incredibly, just a year or so later, she was actually hired by the city as a relocation manager, helping people get out of buildings she determined were unlivable and prosecuting the slumlords who owned them.

With a big heart for helping and a good head for figuring out ways to get slumlords to shape up or ship out, she was good at the job and she loved it. Again, Sister Mary was doing her all to help the poor, those who the system had all but given up on. "Our society was so concerned about *things* and not very concerned about *people*," says Sister Mary. "I saw there were human beings hurting out there, but they were being thrown away by society. I wanted to do something about it."

Since then, the former-teacher-turned-social-activist has kept herself on this side of the bars, but she still is moved to action. In 1986, when homelessness was becoming noticed as a major social issue all across the United States, a study in Louisville showed that the homeless population there was reaching astronomical proportions. In particular, after they were forced to leave the shelters where they slept at night, the city's homeless men had no place to go during the day. The church opened a day shelter, and Sister Mary agreed to run it. "I guess I was the logical choice for the job, being so outspoken and involved with social issues in the city," says Sister Mary. "I figured I could make a big difference."

When she was first offered the job, she thought it would be a great opportunity to help comfort and aid the homeless temporarily, until a permanent solution to end homelessness was found. "I thought we were a strong and intelligent country with plenty of money and resources, so we should have this homeless thing solved in no time," remembers Sister Mary. "At the most I figured I would be working at this job for a few years." Little did she know, she was taking on a job with no discernible end in sight.

Sister Mary won't be nominated for a Nobel Prize anytime soon, although she has received plenty of accolades and awards in Louisville for her service to the homeless. This Samaritan will probably never solve the homeless problem in this country, or even in Louisville. But what she can do is love the people who pass under her shelter's roof like the rest of the world no longer does. "The world has passed judgment on them because of their economic status," explains Sister Mary. "Our priorities are so confused that we associate a person's worth with their wealth or lack of it. Because they are poor and homeless, we cast them out and don't give them the respect that every single human being deserves."

With that compassion in her soul seven days a week, the seventy-year-old nun rises at about 4 A.M. so she can be at the shelter by 5. She makes sure the coffee is hot, the towels are clean, and that there is plenty of soap in the showers for the men to clean up. Most of those she serves are plagued by myriad problems, ranging from drug and alcohol abuse to the long-standing damage done by years of neglect or physical and emotional abuse as children. "Most of the men's problems are rooted deep in their upbringing," insists Sister Mary. "If we don't start caring for our children's hearts and heads, then we will just keep producing homeless people." And every day Sister Mary cares, and every day Sister Mary saves lives.

At the center, these men will be able to feel like human beings for the day. They'll get a shower and a shave, then they'll be able to make phone calls to family or prospective employers. "Most of these men try very hard to get jobs and get their lives back together," says Sister Mary, "but did you ever try to save up for an apartment and have a life on minimum wage? You'd probably be on the street, too."

The center offers the men a variety of resources, including counselors of all types. The facility provides new clothes for their backs and new shoes for their feet. And most of all, it provides kindness, support, and ever-present love. "Some of these men have nobody left out there for them," laments Sister Mary. "We give them free long-distance calls at Christmas, and they have no one to call. They have burned all their bridges with friends and families. But they know they are always welcome here."

Now and again, word comes of someone who made it off the streets because of the program and Sister Mary's love. The word usually comes in the form of a simple thank-you or a note: "You saved my life," reads one. "Thank you for caring," reads another. "You made me realize I was a human being again," says one man. There are the tales of men whose lives were shattered when they lost their wives or families to some unimaginable tragedy, but who have finally regained their hope and happiness enough to stand on their own two feet again.

If Sister Mary Kathleen ever expected *all* these men to heal and move on with their lives, she would certainly have quit by now or lost her mind or her will. In truth, there are many successes, but also many men who are still struggling after years. But still she keeps at it, working not to fix but to comfort, offering gentility instead of judgment, and knowing her efforts will never stop the problem but only aid its victims. "Our priorities and values need to be looked at and rearranged before the homeless issue can ever be solved," says Sister Mary. "It starts in our youth. Instead of teaching our children the value and worth of human life, we buy them $300 tennis shoes and teach them to value things. Instead of teaching love, forgiveness, and compassion, our leaders teach our children to hate and kill each other."

The hard truth is that many of these men will never heal. And although she would love to see all of them happy and healthy, it's not just about getting them off the streets for Sister Mary Kathleen. It's about loving them and letting them know that as long as she is around, these men will not be thrown out, even if they are counted out by society. "I know there are plenty of people who came here who we have helped move up and on," says Sister Mary, "and there will be plenty more I know. But my job is to care for the ones who are still here, whether they ever get off the streets or not."

Sister Mary makes many speeches about success rates and how their efforts are working to help the fight to eradicate homelessness. But in her heart she knows the problem is much deeper than anything she can solve with her program alone. But still, she pushes her heart up a mountain of hope and healing every single day, even though she knows it will just start all over again tomorrow. She is there to care.

"Whenever it comes time to try and raise the money we so badly need to run this place, I have to talk the talk about all our success with turning these men's lives around here, and I can do that well," says Sister Mary, "but those miraculous success stories are few and far between. That's not really the reason we are here. We can't fix the homeless problem by just fixing the victims. It's a much deeper social problem that's going to take this country and the government getting much more involved. But what we can do here is to help, comfort, and love these people, to give them the tools to get back on their feet. Then it's up to them. We are here to try and heal the hurt and give them back their hearts."

Whether homelessness can ever be defeated or not, the victims must be cared for. As Sister Mary Kathleen fights the good fight, she'll keep hope and be inspired by every smile she sees, every "thank-you" she hears, and every face she sees that feels human again, if just for a few hours every day when they are around her. "I love each and every one of them," says Sister Mary, "because they are human beings." And whether they make progress or not, whether they get back on their feet or not, even if they stay exactly where they are, she'll keep caring, because that is what we are supposed to do as human beings. "Jesus taught us to have compassion for everyone, not just those who are successful in life," reminds Sister Mary. "That's the example I'll follow for as long as He gives me the strength to do it."

✳ DR. DOUGLAS STUART: "MOST CHARITY IS SQUANDERED."

DEUT. ⎫ "THERE SHOULD BE
LUKE. ⎭ NO POOR" ⇄ "THE POOR YOU WILL ALWAYS HAVE AMONG YOU" ❗

↪ GIVING TO THE POOR IS NOT LIKE ANY OTHER INVESTMENT. IT IS AN INVESTMENT IN THE DIGNITY OF ANOTHER HUMAN BEING.

CHAPTER NINE

◆ The Principle of Listening

"He who hath ears to hear, let him hear."

—Mark 4:9

Have you ever gotten between two friends who were arguing and tried to work out a compromise? It was probably quite a chore, because they most likely weren't interested in listening to anything but their own point of view. More than a few international crises occur for the same reason—one group of people just doesn't take the time to listen to what another group is really saying. Listening is so easy to do, yet so hard to *remember* to do. But when we make an effort to open our ears, our hearts and heads are soon to follow, making happiness attainable for all.

Chances are, most people don't think of listening as a heroic trait. But those who have trained themselves to hear what others are saying can make miracles happen. Just think of the last time you were hurting physically, mentally, emotionally, or spiritually. The first step you took to get help was probably finding someone to listen to you. How many of your worst days or most emotionally trying periods of your life have been marked by your need to just have someone listen and hear you out? Much of the time we don't even need a smart answer. We just need to know that somebody cares enough to listen.

What Is Listening?

◈ *Listening is the most basic way we as human be-* ings can join and communicate our collective strength, intelligence, and spirit. Instead of operating as separate and competing units, we can use listening to bond together with the rest of mankind in common cooperation. Ultimately, together we are greater than we are alone. Can you imagine a world in which none of us could speak the same language? Can you imagine struggling to understand everything everybody else was saying? Think about how difficult it would be to function as a society, or for any of us to get anything done. Our success is because we can connect to each other, and the way we do that is through listening. Now just think of how much more successful we would be if we understood each other better.

When we listen, we become smarter, happier, and stronger human beings. We become a healthy and helpful part of our world. But when we refuse or fail to do it, it almost always inevitably leads to isolation, impotence, and disaster for us and all those around us.

So often a spat with our mate, trouble at work, feuds with family members, or even much more dramatic and extreme confrontations arise from the failure to genuinely listen to others. So much personal and social strife and unhappiness can be traced back to this rampant inability. From grand events like the sinking of the *Titanic,* the attack on Pearl Harbor, and the Cuban Missile Crisis to the small but no less important of life's tragedies like the unattended cries of a child or the disregard for an elderly relative, not listening is a sure recipe for disaster.

When we don't listen, we separate ourselves from the common consciousness. It's like we unplug our bodies, hearts, and heads from the mainframe of humanity. Once we do that, we are operating alone, with only the power of one instead of the knowledge, spirit, and strength of all we could choose to hear and tap into. We have all met people who have chosen to live this kind of lonely existence. They are usually angry and destructive, and many of them often finally express their frustration in some desperate act against humanity. That is, of course, the worst-case scenario, but there are many more limited cases of such isolation.

But the most important reason to listen to others is simply to love others, which leads to the common joy of society. And listening is one of the best ways to love somebody else, simply by letting them know that you care about what they have to say. By taking the time to listen to others, we send a signal that they are valuable and that their thoughts, desires, and interests are worthy. What we do once that conversational respect is established is a separate matter. But first and foremost, everybody wants to feel that they are worthwhile enough to be listened to by others.

Consider the easiest way to hurt somebody without saying a word or lifting a finger—to ignore them or their comments. This is usually much more painful than insults. Remember how you felt the last time someone gave you the "silent treatment"? Even if you aren't trying to hurt someone, it's easy to accidentally forget to listen. Take, for example, the stereotypical conversation between a man and wife—she wants to vent about her feelings, but he listens only long enough to come up with a solution (not to pick on men, although we do seem to have a little more wax in our ears, especially when a sporting event is on!). This behavior leaves the wife hurt and unsatisfied. Even though he may be hearing and responding to everything she says, she's still hurt because he's really not listening with the fullness of his being. But the failure to listen certainly isn't limited to one gender or the other. So much of the time people just want to talk and know that somebody will spend the time to listen for as long as it takes for them to feel valuable or secure again. It is the attention that is important, not necessarily what we are saying, yet what we are saying must be regarded, otherwise we feel slighted.

So with so much at stake, why do most of us continue to be such bad listeners? Maybe it's because we are all too busy talking. There are reams of self-help books we buy on how to communicate with others that go on forever about how to talk to your spouse, your children, and your boss. But it's amazing how many fewer pages are given to the most important yet most misunderstood part of communication—listening. We all seem to be obsessed with opening our mouths, and we always have something supposedly important and worthwhile to say. It's important to contribute our thoughts to society, but while we are busy shooting off our traps, what are we missing out on? Probably, everything we need to be hearing. Plus, not knowing when to be quiet and listen to the other person is just plain rude to the individual who's forced to listen to our one-sided tirade.

But even when we do take the time to be silent enough to let others talk, are we really hearing what they're saying, or listening just enough to make a smart comment or have a confrontational winning comeback? Worse still, we might listen only so we can use a person's comments to route the conversation immediately back to ourselves. Again, this completely misses most of the point of listening. I call this misguided approach at communication "drive-by dialogue"—we wrap somebody up in a conversation just long enough to shoot off our mouths then leave them wounded by our complete disregard and disinterest in anything they needed to say or wanted to share. This rude behavior is both hurtful and damaging to the individual we are speaking to and to society on the whole, yet so many of us do it every day, often without realizing it.

Genuine listening is looking past ourselves and what we want to say so we might be more open to hearing what's on somebody else's mind and in their heart. It's about focusing on our relationships with others instead of simply on ourselves. When we learn the skills and the restraint needed to listen to others, we are then capable of communicating or expressing our love for them.

How Can I Bring Listening into My Life?

A NICE DESCRIPTION OF LISTENING RATHER THAN JUST HEARING, WHICH IS PHYSIOLOGICAL.

The art of listening is so much more than just a matter of opening our ears and focusing on what the other person is saying. It's about opening our minds and our hearts to the truth, to ideas, and to the people around us and around the world. It's not just hearing the sounds but hearing the signs of what is going on. When most people talk, so often we need to listen between the lines to what they really mean, and more important, what they really need.

We all can learn how to be better listeners and be heroes to our friends, families, countries, and communities if we focus on loving others instead of looking out for our own selfish desires. Much of the time, our egos are too loud to allow us to hear anything else. We must muffle the sound of our own pride and desire long enough to hear others, and then we are ready to listen.

There are three basic parts to listening. First of all, we must open our ears. Making the effort to physically pay attention to someone is crucial, even when we don't necessarily want to because we are too busy, too tired, too lazy, or when we are so

EARS → WE HEAR
MINDS → WE KNOW
HEARTS → WE FEEL

overcome with anger, sadness, or selfishness that we lose control of ourselves. We must physically close our mouths and shut off those egos of ours and simply hear others.

Second, we must open our minds. Really thinking about what we just heard is crucial, regardless of how trivial we think it might be. Real listeners don't let anything just go in one ear and out the other. Only by truly listening with earnest intent can we inherit the information and wisdom of our elders, our teachers, and our peers, so the cycle of social evolution can continue and so we can be intellectually connected to all those in community with us. Without this intellectual devotion to listening, we cannot learn. And without learning, society reverts. Important information is everywhere, buried deep in everything we hear. There really is no such thing as useless chatter. Everything we hear can teach us something about ourselves, others or society and life in general.

And finally, listening is about opening our hearts. Those who need to convey some crucial information about themselves to us might choose to do so not in the words they use but in the way they speak to us. This information will go unheard if we are not sensitive to the signs of another's pain or joy. This means we must listen beyond the information, beyond the capacity of our minds to interpret, relying also on our hearts to understand and empathize with what someone else is feeling.

There is not one person alive who does not need to know how to listen and how to listen better all the time. Every job you can think of benefits from good listening. Your family will benefit, and your friends will, too. And of course you will prosper in the long run, reaping the rewards that loving others by listening to them brings.

If you still don't think good listeners are heroes, take a few moments to listen with your head and your heart to this tale of a high school teacher who became a national hero because she took the time to listen.

HARK THE HERO TEACHER

When Rachel Jupin started teaching in her forties, after a lifetime of overcoming the barriers and battles of life, she knew she could help her students through rough times like the ones she had when she was a kid. But she never realized that her experiences might one day help her save so many lives.

Life was anything but easy for Rachel, growing up in the poverty-ridden projects of New Bedford, Massachusetts. "There was nothing under our tree come Christmastime, because there was just no money or nobody to care to put it there," remembers Rachel.

When she was just nine years old, her father left the family, leaving her, her twin brother, her two sisters, and their mom with not much more than the clothes on their backs. They were broke and hungry, and her mother had no real idea how she was going to support her kids. The pressures of raising her children on her own took its toll on Rachel's mom, distancing her from her children emotionally. "She just didn't make much time for us after that," says Rachel. "Listening to her children's problems just really wasn't high on her list. I never felt like she was there for me when I needed to talk to her."

That's when young Rachel first decided that when she grew up and had children of her own, she would make sure she was always available when they needed her attention and when they just needed someone to listen. "What I wanted more than anything else was to grow up, get married, have lots of kids, and give them a lot of love," says Rachel.

But what Rachel couldn't get from her own parents, she did at least get from her aunt Laureate. "I could tell Aunt Laureate anything," remembers Rachel fondly. "She always had the time to listen. If it wasn't for her, I don't know what would have happened to me."

With Aunt Laureate's attention, Rachel stayed out of trouble and made it through high school. After graduation, she went to work for a telephone company. There she met a telephone repairman, and the two married soon after. Rachel quickly realized her dream of having lots of kids—four sons and two daughters to be exact. And she gave them all the love and attention she didn't get when she was growing up. "I always made it a point to spend a great deal of time with my kids," remembers Rachel. "I became very involved in their lives and especially in their education. I wanted to make sure they were getting the kind of attention that kids need and that I never got from my parents. I never wanted my kids to need to turn to someone else because I wasn't there for them."

Rachel loved her children, her family, and being a full-time mom. But when times got tough financially for the family, she needed to find a job to help out. Leaving the house and her kids for any part of the day to work outside was the last thing she ever wanted to do. But her kids were growing up, and the family was strapped. "You do what you've got to do," says Rachel. "I would just have to make the time to do two jobs and do them both well."

She searched the want ads for a job, trying to find something she might enjoy. Rachel always loved literature. She'd spend hours each day reading to her children to teach them to read better, and in the back of her mind she always toyed with the idea of one day becoming a writer. So when she heard about a reporter position opening at a newspaper in nearby Boston, she jumped at it. Rachel loved the job, and she was good at it. In fact, a few years later she decided to enroll in college at night so she could get a degree in writing.

But suddenly, she hit a bump in the road when a routine doctor's checkup found she had breast cancer. "That was a very difficult period for me," says Rachel. "But I had a lot of support from my family and friends. I always had people in my corner who I could talk to. And I think I was so busy focusing on all the things I had to do and people I needed to take care of that it got me through."

With her family behind her all the way, Rachel beat the cancer, and in June of 1995, she graduated *magna cum laude* from the University of Massachusetts at Dartmouth with a degree in

English writing and communication. She started thinking about how to put her degree to use and then it hit her. She loved kids and was always so involved in her own kids' education, why not become a teacher?

Rachel went back to school to earn her Master's degree. After graduating in 2000, she applied for a job in her hometown of New Bedford teaching kids who were growing up in the same tough conditions and dire straits she had. "I can really identify with the struggles a lot of these kids have to go through," says Rachel. "A great number of them face financial hardships that send them to bed hungry at night. Or some of them have so many problems at home with their parents that they can't even stay at home anymore, so they are living on friends' couches, just trying to survive. It's tough to concentrate on Shakespeare when you are worrying about a roof over your head."

From the moment she entered the classroom, Rachel knew she had her work cut out for her as a teacher, disciplinarian, surrogate mom, and sometimes even referee. One day, a fight broke out in her classroom. When she got in between the battling boys and tried to break it up, one of them socked her right in the jaw. "That was a rude awakening to the kind of situations I was dealing with," says Rachel. "There were some troubled kids in there, and they needed a lot more than just a good education." What Rachel realized they needed most was someone to care, to discipline them, and to listen to what they were going through.

So Rachel became even more determined to be a stabilizing and disciplining force at the school, bringing order and compassion to the troubled students. She put her thinking cap on to come up with ideas to inspire the kids in the classroom, such as teaching them Homer's *Odyssey* by having them report on it like newscasters—complete with a chance to film it at a nearby TV station. And she turned on her heart to help her students outside the classroom, letting everyone know that she was ready to help and ready to listen to anyone who needed to talk.

The students came to her in droves. There was the poor but bright freshman boy who loved Rachel's class and had a knack for poetry. She supported his efforts, and he went on to win a prize for his writing. In another case, a young girl confided in Rachel that she was being physically abused. Rachel was there to listen, comfort, and try to assist the teen, eventually convincing the girl to get help. And when a young girl writing an essay in her class on personal heroes wrote that she had none because she had "nobody except herself to depend on," Rachel filled in as her hero. Bouncing from one foster home to another, the troubled teen desperately wanted someplace stable to stay where she could feel like a normal teenage girl for a little while. Rachel offered her own home as a sanctuary from the storm.

But that wasn't the first time Rachel's home was a refuge for troubled students. On any given night of the week, at least one student could be found at her house—sometimes getting help with homework, but other times just talking to their favorite teacher. Rachel says the kids often told her that she was the only person who they felt was willing to really listen to them and their problems. "I don't feel special for doing that," says Rachel.

"I believe we all need to learn how to listen to our children more. They have a lot to say about what they are going through and what they need. We can prevent a lot of problems and do a lot of good if we take the time to hear what they are trying so hard to tell us."

Listening to all her students, but especially the troubled ones, is how she came to know Amy, a senior in her writing for college class. Most students thought Amy was just an average teenager with a gift for gab. But unbeknown to them, the rugged ROTC student came from a troubled household, and underneath her happy-go-lucky exterior was a firestorm of pain and confusion.

Amy took an immediate liking to Rachel because she could talk to her about everything and anything that was on her mind. "She started coming in after school just to shoot the breeze about life at school and the class," says Rachel. But it wasn't long before Amy was sticking like glue to Rachel's side, bending her ear whenever she could and sharing some deeply personal problems. "She was there all the time," remembers Rachel, "before school, after school, and lunch, too. It seemed like every time I turned around, there she was. Each time we'd talk she would tell me a little more about how hard her life was at home and how it was affecting her." It didn't take long for Rachel to realize how troubled Amy was, and that the best thing she could do for the girl was just to let her know she was always there to listen.

At times, Amy was so disturbed by her life at home that she'd ask Rachel if she could come home with her instead. So from time to time, Rachel invited her over for dinner. After enjoying a home-cooked meal and the wholesome serving of the loving family life she was starving for, the two would sit together in the living room, where Amy would unload all her worries and Rachel would listen. "She didn't have much guidance in her life at all," says Rachel. "But most important, there was nobody who cared about anything she had to say. I really knew how she felt after growing up the way I did, and so I figured the best thing I could do was just to let her know I was really interested in listening to whatever she had to say."

When Amy asked Rachel if she could start going to church with her, Rachel happily obliged. Soon, Amy was spending many a Sunday with Rachel after services, just sharing her thoughts. As Rachel became more and more of Amy's confidante, soon there was nothing Amy wouldn't talk with her about. She spoke about her boyfriends and her pals at school; she told Rachel of her plans to join the military after high school. Amy shared all her dreams and her aspirations, her fears and her trepidations. In the middle of her senior year, when Amy moved to a different part of town and was forced to change schools because she was living too far away to commute, Rachel was one of the first she confided in. Amy was devastated, weeping at the thought of leaving the teacher she loved. But there was still church and plenty of time to see each other on the weekends. And Rachel let her know that she would still always be there to listen.

But Rachel didn't always know what was true and what was

fantasy when Amy talked. There was the time Amy told Rachel she was getting married to the boy she had a crush on, a boy Rachel didn't approve of very much because of his rebellious and disinterested attitude at school. But Rachel knew something very real was wrong when Amy showed up for church one day with her head shaved. "I knew she was trying to tell me something when she did that," says Rachel, "but I also knew I wasn't going to be able to force anything out of her. I just had to listen carefully and hope she would eventually tell me what was wrong like she always did."

Soon after that, on Rachel's birthday, instead of expecting a gift, the devoted teacher gave Amy a present. It was a guardian angel pin. Rachel didn't know everything that was going on in Amy's life, but she thought the young girl could use all the help she could get. "I told her it should remind her that angels are always watching over us," says Rachel. "I thought she needed it more than I did right then."

What Rachel couldn't know is that the gift came at a time when Amy was wrestling with a big decision that would change her life and the fate of many others for years to come. It was something that she wanted to share badly with Rachel, but she didn't know how to talk about it. "It was obvious that she was dying to get something out, and I could tell it was something important," says Rachel, "but it was as if she didn't know how to say it, and it was killing her. I just had to pay really close attention. Then maybe I could eventually piece it together, or maybe she would finally just blurt out whatever it was."

Slowly Amy began to share bits of information with Rachel through broken sentences and incomplete thoughts—tantalizing tidbits of something big, something that was going to happen soon. Rachel hung on every word, while trying not to pressure her for fear of scaring her off. But it soon became eerily apparent to Rachel that Amy wasn't just trying to tell her something important about herself; she was warning the teacher who took the time to listen, the only adult who she really believed loved her, that something ominous was about to happen. "She still wouldn't tell me what it was," remembers Rachel, "but she was terrified of divulging something awful, and, she was obviously in a great deal of pain because of it." But still, Rachel had no way to force the issue. All she could do was keep the lines of communication open and keep being there for her young friend in turmoil.

Then, just days before Thanksgiving, Amy finally got up the nerve to divulge the unthinkable—something that Rachel never could have imagined in a million years. Amy told her teacher that she and several classmates were planning a Columbine-style massacre to murder as many of the school's 3,250 students as they could. She was telling Rachel, she said, because she didn't want anything to happen to her. "It was the most horrifying thing I ever heard," recalls Rachel. "Of all the things I could have expected her to say, this wasn't one of them. I knew immediately this was big, and I had to call the authorities."

With Rachel's support, Amy told police of she and her five friends' mind-numbing plan to sneak into school armed with an arsenal of guns hidden under black trench coats, running through the halls and slaughtering everyone they saw. Then, police say, she told them they planned to shoot each other on the roof of the school after getting drunk and high on marijuana and acid. Amy reportedly had originally agreed to get them guns, but now she wanted out—not because she was afraid for her own life, but because she didn't want anything to happen to Rachel.

It was something straight out of tomorrow's horrible headlines, but it hadn't happened yet. And they could still stop it.

As authorities went to work investigating the terrifying claim and interviewing suspects named by Amy, Rachel kept Amy closer than ever. She kept reassuring Amy, letting the girl know that she could tell her anything and that she would do all she could to protect her. "I know she believed that those kids might kill her for telling me," says Rachel, "and she also realized that I would need to report this, so she knew she could get into a lot of trouble, too. But she came forward anyway."

That Thanksgiving Rachel invited Amy over to dine with her and her family. Before sitting down to eat, Amy frantically informed Rachel that she feared the attack would happen any day. Together they called authorities. Within hours, the alleged conspirators were arrested.

Five days later, Amy was also arrested and arraigned on conspiracy charges. It was an outcome she knew was possible, but something she had to risk to save her teacher. When police asked Amy why she came forward, she told them point-blank it was to save Rachel, the teacher who was always there to listen, the only adult, she told police, who she believed really loved her. She told police that she thought of Rachel like a mother and that she was willing to do whatever it took to keep Rachel safe, even if it meant personally protecting her in the massacre.

As Amy stood before the judge, trembling at the thought of facing many years behind bars for her involvement, she clutched the guardian angel pin Rachel gave her to protect her. "I told her to just hold on to her guardian angel and everything will be fine," says Rachel. "Everyone is calling me a hero, but she's the one who came forward. She knew the risks of telling me, and she still did it. I know she was a very confused little girl, and obviously she shouldn't have taken up with those other kids in the first place. But the bottom line is that she saved the school."

Undoubtedly, there isn't a parent of one child at New Bedford High who isn't grateful that Amy did the right thing and told someone about the impending catastrophe. But without Rachel there to listen, Amy's warning might have fallen on a deaf ear or never even have happened at all. "I will always be there for Amy," says Rachel, "and for any other child who needs someone to listen."

CHAPTER TEN

◆ The Principle of Forgiveness

To err is human, to forgive divine."

—Alexander Pope

◈ *"Forgive and forget." "Don't hold a grudge."* I remember hearing both those bits of advice quite often when I was growing up, don't you? Yet the concept of forgiveness doesn't get much attention nowadays. How often do we turn on the evening news or open the daily paper and see a major headline story about one nation, group, or individual forgiving another for some transgression? And how often do we consider forgiveness in our own lives as a way of resolving differences with others? It's not very often in either case.

Although most countries acknowledge that war is not the answer and that peaceful cohabitation is the goal, one of the strongest components of peace—forgiveness—is almost entirely abandoned in international relations. And although most people agree in theory that strife and hatred is not a positive perspective on life, how often do we step up to the reconciliatory plate and practice forgiveness when life puts us to the test?

With all the stories we hear of war, domestic crime, and personal feuds, doesn't it seem odd that we rarely discuss in our public forums the idea of finding resolution for all these disagreements by one or both of the parties forgiving each other? That's not to say we should endorse forgiveness as a replacement for the enforcement of law or the necessary element of incarceration to protect others from criminals. And likewise, a nation must defend itself against transgressions by warring neighbors. But after such legal or defensive measures are taken, don't our leaders and our cultures seem to be obsessed with the concept of retribution and punishment? This is a dangerous road to travel for two very important reasons. First of all, it simply continues the cycle of hatred from one generation to another, making it impossible for resolution and peace to ever occur. And it teaches our children to continue the violence in their own generation. Do we really want them to believe that we must all excise a pound of flesh from our neighbor for wrongs acted against us?

What Is Forgiveness?

See Michael Martin's Definitions

*Forgiveness is one of the most powerful and im-*portant threads of civilizations. And it is a heroic value, which makes miracles possible for those who practice and those who receive it. Forgiveness is the ability to pardon another person's wrongs or injustices against us, and it's a necessary attribute in an imperfect world.

This doesn't mean we should ever approve or invite inappropriate or hurtful actions against us. And there is nothing inhumane about requiring the culprits of such acts to make reparations for their activities or to be held accountable. But at some point, we must be willing to let go of the pain and hatred we have for the individual who committed the act and move on. Otherwise, we will all almost certainly be extracting revenge from each other for the rest of time, each sequential act of vengeance trapping us in a pendulumlike sequence of hate. There simply is no reasonable way to demand pure justice in our imperfect world. We must be willing to reset the tables of justice so we can all start fresh and try to do better next time. Forgiveness is the pardoning or healing of rifts that is necessary in our world to make that kind of second chance possible for us all.

It's not like the concept of forgiveness is a brand-new idea. It's been around for centuries, and it has been espoused by leaders and thinkers throughout history. Forgiveness was advocated by just about very other enlightened spiritual leader throughout time. And look at the reams of clinical psychological data showing the adverse effects of holding a grudge and the revitalizing power of forgiveness. Psychologists will tell you that an unforgiving nature produces trauma and stress, and doctors will tell you that the effects of failing to forgive can be as far-reaching and deleterious as heart disease, ulcers, and even stroke. If that's the reward for failing to forgive, it seems obvious that forgiveness might be a healthy and winning strategy for everyone involved.

Also, consider the tremendous effort necessary to navigate through a world filled with those who hate. The unavoidable result of such a life is the constant need to look over your shoulder to see which foe is coming after you next. With every altercation comes another new web of confrontation and suffering as you make more and more enemies. Eventually, the world becomes a jungle filled with danger around every corner. At that point, it really no longer matters who was wrong or right or what the altercation was even about. You are now the victim of your own failure to forgive, and there is no way to ever win in that scenario or type of world. The only result of such an existence is unhappiness.

But beyond the personal value of forgiveness, consider one's responsibility to forgive as part of the commitment and desire to love others. Surely, it is easier to give in to the desire for revenge and refuse to take the time and effort to find reconciliation. But then you are killing that individual's ability to reform and change their life. This takes away their God-given right to seek emotional and spiritual rejuvenation and rebirth by making amends.

The failure to forgive also results ultimately in a tremendous burden on society. Until you extend forgiveness to someone who has truly wronged you, the offending individual can never fully reform and become a healthy contributing hero in their own right. So the selfish act of "holding a grudge" blocks all the goodness that a reformed person could do in the long run. By taking away their divine right to change their ways, you take away their potential to help the world around them. For every person that they hurt now or they fail to help, you share some portion of responsibility. Now do the math and figure out just how much harm your selfish act of failing to forgive can cause. It's exponential!

How Can I Bring Forgiveness into My Life?

◈ *The failure to forgive spawns hatred, animosity, and* anger. But because we are all designed to love each other, and the proliferation of love brings us joy in the long run, obviously the more relationships we have that are centered around hate or estrangement, the less happiness we have. We live in a complex and harried world. Most of us encounter so many people and problems during the course of our day and our lives. It's tough enough getting through our lives without the added frustration of somebody getting in our way and slighting us. When somebody does, it just seems a whole lot easier to hate them and take action against them or banish them from our lives than to try and resolve the issue and shake hands, right? Wrong. In the long run, that forgiveness is actually the most beneficial thing we can do for ourselves and the rest of

175

society. So now let's look beyond the negative ramifications of not forgiving to the wondrous world of forgiveness and what it makes possible.

Take, for example, the story of Deacon Martin G. Towey. A week before Easter, his daughter was viciously murdered by an eighteen-year-old burglar. Her body was dumped in the woods, and the murderer bragged about it to friends. The murderer was eventually caught and brought to justice, yet when it came time for sentencing and punishment to be doled out, Martin vehemently opposed sending his daughter's murderer to the death chamber. He even sent a letter to the murderer in prison forgiving him for his action.

"After sending the letter, it was like a great weight was lifted off my shoulders," says Martin. "It was like I suddenly became a better, more responsible and caring father, husband, teacher, and deacon because of it. I knew I had to get that hatred out of my soul to move on. I only hope my forgiveness did as much good for him as it did for me and my family."

But all that being said, the hatred and anger that emanate from some action taken against us or a loved one is, at times, hard to suppress. It takes great heroic strength and willpower to realize that although our immediate desire may be to destroy or harm the person who offended us, it serves our best interest and the interest of society to forgive. But just like all other base instincts designed only to serve us in the short run, the desire for revenge is so strong at times that it sometimes overcomes us. So how do we prevent those emotions from taking over our thoughts and actions? How do we replace hatred with the desire and commitment to forgive?

Reflecting on all the different reasons why forgiveness is more beneficial can help you find the strength to forgive. But ultimately, the greatest way to inspire yourself to forgive is by focusing on the humanity and divinity in others and in yourself. Once you see others and yourself as beautiful beings worthy of love, despite all our imperfections, you'll be more apt to forgive. Eventually, the cycle of forgiveness you start will help stop the cycle of hate that probably led to the hurtful act against you in the first place.

One such case is the remarkable story of a young and misled military man who got so drunk, high, and depressed one night that he stupidly ended another man's life for money. But more extraordinary than the senselessness of his act was the sensibility and sensitivity of the family who forgave him.

MERCY FOR MURDER

Billy Neal Moore was driving home from the scene of the crime with $5,600 in stolen cash when the booze and the drugs started to wear off. That's when it really hit him—he had just shot and killed a man. "I had killed somebody for money," remembers Billy. "It was like one of those horrible nightmares that you wake up screamin' from. But I couldn't wake up from this one."

The twenty-two-year-old soldier stationed at Fort Gordon, Georgia, still couldn't believe what he had done. Indeed, it all seemed like some kind of bad dream, but it was all too real, just like the wad of cash stuffed in his pocket and the gunpowder residue left on his hands from the .38-caliber smoking pistol he used to kill seventy-seven-year-old Fredger Stapelton. Now all he could do was run and try to hide from the horrible crime he had just committed. But where could he go? There was no place on earth he could escape from his crime and his conscience. "A man was dead and I killed him. I pulled the trigger," explains Billy. "I knew it was just a matter of time before they found me, so I just went back home and waited for the sheriff to come for me."

How on earth did his life come to this? he frantically wondered as he raced home. Billy had a tough childhood and had been in a few mishaps with the law when he was just a kid and before he joined the Army to straighten himself out, but certainly nothing like this.

Billy hadn't been very happy the week leading up to that fateful night. His wife had called him from New York and told him she was leaving him to return to Germany, where they were stationed the year before, leaving the couple's three-year-old boy in Billy's care. Money was tight, his wife was gone, and Billy was angry and hurting. The misguided young man tried to kill the pain one night with drugs and alcohol. "I was in a very bad place back then," remembers Billy. "I was so upset with her for what she did to me and to my little boy. And the booze just made me feel more isolated and alone."

On that April night in 1974, the confused young man and an

Army buddy got filthy drunk on a fifth of Jack Daniel's and a bottle of wine before lighting up joints. Then they hatched a plan—ripping off an old man who lived nearby. The man didn't trust banks, and he had $20,000 stashed away in his closet. They figured they could just break in, take the money, and run. "Nobody was going to get hurt," says Billy. "All we had to do was walk in and walk out."

Mired in self-pity, pain, and under the influence, young Billy latched onto the idea of what was supposed to be a simple robbery. "Somehow I guess I convinced myself that this terrible idea would work out," says Billy. "But any time you set out to do something that you know in your heart is wrong, it leads you down the road to a place you never think you are going to wind up, hurting people in ways you never could have imagined." Somewhere in the haze of it all, Billy made another bad decision. On the way out the door, he picked up his pistol and loaded it on the way.

Barely able to drive, the two men made the long haul down the interstate to the town almost an hour away where the old man lived. They broke into the house through a window and quickly found the stash of cash. But when they only found $5,600, they kept looking. That's when they ran smack into the resident of the house, Fredger Stapelton, who was pointing a shotgun right at them. As Billy tried to run, the old man started shooting. Then Billy made yet another terrible decision—the worst decision yet—he fired back, shooting the old man in the chest and killing him almost instantly.

Billy doesn't remember a whole lot more of what happened during the minutes that followed that horrible act, except that he started on that long drive home to Augusta. That's where he first sobered up enough to realize that he had committed murder—and for $5,600! "It was playing like a movie in my head," remembers Billy. "I just wanted to stop it, but I couldn't. It was happening over and over again inside my brain."

Once Billy made it home, he didn't have much of a chance to think about it too much longer before a knock came at the door. He peered fearfully out the door to see who it was. His worst fears were confirmed. It was the sheriff, and he had Billy's partner with him.

"I felt so ashamed and cold all over," remembers Billy. "But there was no way I could deny anything. He was there, and he told them I'd done it. Besides, the guilt was killing me anyway. So I just confessed right then and there and handed over the money and the pistol I shot him with." The sheriff hauled Billy into the police station, where he unexpectedly came face to face with the family of the man he had just killed. Again the guilt rushed back into his heart. It was more than he could stand, and he had to do something about it. As he was rushed by them on his way to the holding cell, he caught the eye of a young girl who was crying and he opened up his heart in remorse. "I said, 'I'm truly sorry. I didn't mean for the murder to happen. I meant to rob him, but the murder, I didn't mean for that to happen.' I know now that probably wasn't something that was going to comfort somebody who just lost a loved one. I didn't expect them to forgive me for what I'd done, but I knew I had to say I was sorry."

But little did Billy know that with his heartfelt apology he had planted the seeds of a miracle. The young girl who he spoke to was the old man's niece. And the impression he made on her that night would stay with her for years to come. "There was just something about the way he looked right into my eyes when he apologized," says the victim's niece, Sarah. "I knew that if he could have taken it back he would have."

Because Billy had already confessed to the crime, there was no need for a trial. Justice was swift in the small Georgia town, and less than three months later, on July 17, 1974, he was sentenced in a tiny courtroom with no jury and no fanfare. "William Neal Moore, you are hereby sentenced to die in the electric chair on Friday, September 13, 1974." The words echoed like thunder in Billy's head. As the judge's gavel fell, so did Billy's heart and any hope for the future.

Billy had less than two months to live, but for all intents and purposes, he was already dead. "It was like on TV when you see something like that happen and everything is in slow motion. I could see and hear everything, but it was like it wasn't real anymore. I wasn't really there. I was already gone when he passed that sentence. When that sentence gets passed, your life is already over."

That night, as Billy sat in his cell, he decided to commit suicide. "I thought I might as well go ahead and do it myself instead of waiting for the state to do it their way," says Billy. But that's when he said he heard God's loving voice for the first time. "He told me, 'This is the same thing you did to get in here, and you're sorry you did that, aren't you?' I promised God that night that if I died, the state would have to kill me."

But Billy's life wasn't over yet. There was one man who still saw a little life left in the convicted murderer. That man was a minister named Nealon Guthrie from Ohio. Guthrie heard about Billy's plight from Billy's cousin, who lived in Ohio. He came to Georgia with his wife to comfort Billy in his dying days and to tell him that God would forgive him and welcome him with an open heart when it came time to meet his maker. But for Billy, the minister offered so much more than last rites. His promise of forgiveness offered the beginning of a new life. "You could feel the love just flowing out of these people," says Billy. "And when they told me that Jesus loved me and that he was willing to forgive me for what I had done if I was ready to ask for forgiveness, something changed inside of me."

Billy was overcome with a feeling that he can only describe as rebirth. He immediately agreed to let the minister baptize him right there in the jail in an old bathtub on the porch. "I was about to die, yet it was strange because I never felt more alive in my whole life."

The minister's mission was done, but Billy's journey had just begun. As he headed back to his cell, a feeling came over him that he couldn't describe. He knew what he had to do next. He immediately began writing letters to several members of the victim's family, including the niece he had apologized to the night of the murder. He told them he was genuinely sorry for what he'd done, and he asked them if they could ever find it in their hearts to forgive him. "I was just hopin' they would at least read the letters," recalls Billy, "but I never really expected them to respond. I even said that I understood if they decided not to forgive me, because I probably wouldn't forgive me either if I was in their shoes. But I wanted them to know that I was sorry." He closed each letter by promising to pray for their family that they might have the strength to overcome the tragedy that he had caused.

What happened next was nothing Billy ever could have imagined. Within a few weeks, he had received letters back from almost every member of the family. Not only did they unanimously forgive him for his heinous crime, but several family members even promised to pray for him and to write to him in the future. "There was such an unbelievable sense of peace and love in their hearts that they expressed in those letters," says Billy. "It was like nothing I had ever experienced from anyone I wronged before." The miraculous gesture jump-started Billy's desire to live. "After I shot that man, I felt a part of them died with him, and I was the cause of that," remembers Billy. "So there was all this death inside of me. But when they forgave me, it was like they decided to live again. That made me feel like maybe I could live again, too. I decided right then and there that I wanted to stay alive and use my life to help people."

Billy didn't know how he was going to help yet, but the seeds of service, love, and life were now growing inside of him. Amazingly, a few days after the family forgave him, his first stay of execution was granted. Billy knew the appeals couldn't go on forever, but somehow now he had the most irresistible feeling that his destiny was something other than dying in the electric chair. "I just knew I was supposed to do something important with my life," says Billy. "I was supposed to help people so I could give back some of that love that God and the family had showed me and the love I took away from them."

Billy worked hard to keep his word. With Minister Guthrie's help, Billy enrolled in a Bible study program by mail. He learned more about a kinder and gentle way of living—a lifestyle predicated on loving your neighbor as yourself and loving yourself enough to respect your neighbors. While his lawyers waged the lengthy process of appeals, Billy began to stand up for himself and his newfound values. He immediately began studying the law so he could understand what his lawyers were doing and help them keep him alive. Now Billy knew he had a mission, and he had to stay alive to complete it.

Three years after being arrested, Billy was transferred out of his tiny cell at the county jailhouse to death row at the state penitentiary at Reidsville. There, Billy continued to study law and the Bible. Soon, he began spreading his new way of looking at life to other cellmates, hard-core murderers thought to be well beyond rehabilitation or remorse. But Billy was softening their hearts. He started conducting daily services and Bible studies for a dozen or so inmates on death row and turning killers into caring human beings. "There were men coming to study the Bible with me who even the guards were afraid of at first," says Billy. "But once they realized that the power of forgiveness offered them a chance to change their ways and make a new life, they became loving human beings."

As his preaching grew so did his relationship with the family who forgave him. They exchanged positive and inspiring letters with each other several times a year. Soon the family even began to visit him in prison. With each visit, they would urge him on in his bid to help others and to stay alive himself. And he would try to give back to them a little piece of the love and inspiration he felt he had taken away. "If I could help them with a kind word or some advice based on the wisdom I was learning from my studies," explains Billy, "that was my way of starting to heal the hurt and rebuild what I had destroyed that night."

Meanwhile, as the family continued to write letters to Billy, bolstering his spirit, he began writing articles for religious and spiritual magazines, attempting to inspire the spirit of others with the wisdom and lessons he had learned. He wrote of repentance, forgiveness, and how to transform a wayward life to a (riotous) one. Coming from a man on death row, his words carried a great deal of weight. Before he knew it, Billy was getting letters from hundreds of people across the country every month. They'd read his articles, and they wanted guidance and advice in their struggles with staying on the straight and narrow. Parents of troubled teens wrote asking him for help keeping their sons out of gangs, their daughters from getting pregnant, or their kids off drugs. Billy always responded with answers and support.

He was saving lives and souls from behind bars with the stroke of his pen, spreading the spirit and power of forgiveness and love to thousands of readers. "Somehow, suddenly God gave me the knowledge to help people," says Billy. "I had to keep working for it by studying and praying, but it was forgiveness that gave me the sense of self-worth to even try."

Now Billy knew more than ever that he had to live so he could keep making a difference by helping others. It was the only thing that made sense, the only way to try to make up for what he had done. "There are so many people out there who are hurting and confused," says Billy, "and I wanted to do whatever I could to help. But I had to stick around so I could do that. What good would my life be if it ended just when I realized how to make it mean something for others?"

Billy stepped up his studies of the law so he could do everything in his power to stay alive. But the one thing he wouldn't do is to let his lawyers ask the victims' family to help his case in any way, even after they told him they were behind him 100 percent. "My lawyers were pretty frustrated with me," reveals Billy, "because they knew that the victim's family's support would be a big help in trying to get a reprieve." In fact, when his lawyers told him of their plan to ask the family of the victim to speak on his behalf at a hearing, he refused to allow it. "Their forgiveness was the greatest and purest gift they could have given me," says Billy. "I didn't want that kindness being used to try and save my life now. I didn't believe I had the right to ask anything more of them than they had already given me. I had to give back to them, not the other way around."

But keeping Billy alive was getting increasingly more difficult. As an admitted killer, his lawyers had no trial data or even the possibility of innocence to use as a bargaining chip in the process. All they could do is continue filing appeals and point to Billy's transformation and work behind bars as a reasonable justification for sparing his life.

Continually inspired by the support of the victim's family, Billy continued to inspire and uplift others from behind bars. Over the next few years, many prisoners wrote praises of their conversion at his hands. Amazingly, even though he refused to ask the family to help him in his bid to live, they took it upon themselves to lobby on his behalf. Fredger's young niece, Sarah, who Billy had touched the night of the murder with his apology, was now all grown up and writing letter after letter to the parole board, asking for leniency on his behalf. "He was so young still with so much potential to help so many people out there who could learn from his mistakes and from his repentance," says Sarah. "If you kill a man, he has no chance to do any good. Then there is only the pain and suffering he caused. But if you let him live, he can contribute in some way. I never believed in the death penalty, and I wasn't going to change my mind just because I was the victim of a crime."

Back at the penitentiary, Billy watched as one by one his cellmates went to the electric chair, praying with each one before their time came for hope and salvation and realizing his own time was running out. After a while, the cruel and torturous process became a familiar routine to Billy. Yet each time a cell-mate died, it made Billy that much more resolved to live and do all he could to make others see the senselessness of this system. "If you kill people, they have no opportunity to ever ask forgiveness of their victims," insists Billy. It is a system that robs people not only of their lives but of their chance to repent and repay the world for their crimes by helping others. "Then they can never change," says Billy. "They can never make a difference and help anyone if they're dead. All that does is keep the pain, hatred, and death going on over and over again."

As time crept by, Billy used his days wisely. He wrote more articles and kept reaching out to more and more people with his words and letters. Three years later, he was transferred again to death row's new location in Jackson. That's where Billy would stay for the next decade, fighting and filing appeal after appeal while helping as many disheartened souls as he could to find a better way to live and love. The years went slow, but his good works kept him busy and kept his mind off the execution that was constantly looming over his head. He started an actual prison ministry on death row, for which he was commended by the prison. The cornerstone of his preaching was that Jesus loved everyone and would forgive anyone for their crimes if they were sincerely sorry and asked for forgiveness. Some of those men even wrote letters of apology to their victim's families asking for their forgiveness. The power of forgiveness in Billy's world was very real.

By August 22, 1990, Billy had exhausted all his appeals, including an appeal to the Georgia Supreme Court. It was the end of the road. Despite all his good works and his extraordinary change of heart, Billy Neal Moore was to be executed at the stroke of midnight.

But the power of forgiveness was about to reach a level that would even astonish Billy. As he sat in his cell, fewer than twelve hours away from that final walk to the electric chair, members of the victim's family were packing for the long trip to the prison. And leading the charge was none other than a sweet, soft-spoken young woman named Sarah, the victim's niece. "We already had one man murdered," remembers Sarah. "So we didn't need another man killed, especially a man like Billy." She was determined not to let Billy die, and she'd convinced all her cousins and aunts and uncles to help fight for his life. "He had truly changed during all those years," says Sarah. "The letters he wrote to me were filled with prayers and lots of genuine love and understanding. Killing that man would have been another crime."

With picket signs and petitions, they made their way to the parole board meeting, which was convened for one last time to consider whether Billy's sentence should be commuted. The merciful mob would accept only one outcome—life instead of death for Billy Moore. It was hope's last stand.

Meanwhile, the power of forgiveness had made its way around the world and back again. A message sent by Jesuit priest Father Deere to Mother Teresa describing Billy's tremendous transformation behind bars so moved the holy woman that she herself called the parole board with just one simple request: she asked them to "do what Jesus would do" if he was in their positions.

At 6 o'clock that evening, just a few hours before he was scheduled to die, Billy was watching TV when a news flash came across the screen. "The parole board today decided to commute the death sentence of William Neal Moore to life in prison," said the anchorman, and just like that Billy Moore was spared execution. He would not be killed today, nor ever would he be placed in the death chamber. "There is no other way to describe the feeling you have when you have been given back your life," says Billy. But there was still yet another miracle in store for Billy. In November 1991, after seventeen years on death row, Billy Neal Moore was released from prison on parole. "It's impossible to describe that day," says Billy, "but in a strange way I felt like I had already been given back my life and my freedom years earlier when I asked for forgiveness and was granted it."

After his release, Billy moved to Illinois, where he was officially ordained as a minister. It was there he met his future wife, Donna Jacks, mother of three who lost her first husband to cancer ironically the same year Billy was supposed to die. They married in 1992 and moved back to Georgia, where Billy now works as an assistant pastor.

Nowadays he crisscrosses the country, speaking at literally hundreds of churches, institutions, and prestigious colleges like

Harvard, Yale, and the University of North Carolina–Chapel Hill on issues of violence, crime, the senselessness of the death penalty, and the crucial role of forgiveness. "Forgiveness is not an emotion or reaction," says Billy. "It's a decision to love even your enemies. And it's the only sensible way to live."